Someone Please Help Me: So I Did

Sharon Fitzmaurice

ACKNOWLEDGEMENTS

Where do you start when you want to thank so many people that have helped shape your life!? To all the people that have been part of my journey and have touched my heart, there are not enough ways to say thank you, but I will try.

Firstly to my wonderful husband John, my children Matthew and Alannah, thank you for having patience with me whilst I hogged the laptop and the dining room table for so many days and nights whilst writing this book, in having patience to listen to my thoughts and feelings about all that I was writing, your words of encouragement and sometimes humour in telling me not to take myself so seriously! You are all such a huge part of my story and always will be, who knows where the next chapter will lead us all.

To my Mother and siblings, thank you for allowing me the space to write my story and my truth. I respect and love you all, there were times when I doubted myself and wanted to hide away from my truth, but I now have the courage and strength to let go of the past hurts and let our healing truly be part of my life.

To my friends, too many of you to mention by name, that would be a whole book in itself. Some I have mentioned in this book, others I hold in my heart knowing that your connection in my life has made a huge difference and one I am very grateful for each and every day. Thank you for seeing the real me.

To all the people that have followed and connected with me over the years through my work and on social media, some we may not have met face to face, but your input into my work and my life has helped me get through many a dark day. This connection is just as important as the physical ones and has helped me share my story.

To my amazing clients and participants of my groups, workshops and retreats, every day I have learned from your amazing courage. I am honoured that you chose me to be part of your journey.

To Phil Noone, thank you for being the first person to read my manuscript, I will always be grateful to you for your honest feedback and comments. What

I will always remember is the beautiful words you wrote after you finished it, you told me that you could feel my personality, my sense of justice, honesty and passion for life throughout the whole book, coming from someone I have never met, meant the world to me.

To Dr. Rebecca Housel who writes from her heart, has honoured me by reading my book and giving me a beautiful review, forever grateful.

To Vanessa Mooney, the amazingly talented graphic designer who created the powerful cover design, she captured all aspects of my personality in wonderful colour and imagination. It still takes my breath away. Thank you

And to my past self, I thank you for having the courage to keep going one day at a time and for allowing yourself to grow in to me. I am looking forward to the journey ahead.

Love Sharon (SK)

Contents

Contents Cont.

INTRODUCTION

Like our lives, our stories are forever changing. Our start in life remains the same but we can always change the next chapter. We are all just finding our way and we all need help at some point in our lives and I am no exception. I started writing this book in my head many years ago, wanting to change each chapter as it happened. Like this book, I have grown and evolved over time.

The storyline that I started out with in my life wasn't always that pleasant and as a child I wanted the happy ending. In my mind, the confusion of not understanding or knowing how to control the situations around me led me to believe that I had no control over anything, even my own mind. For many years I lived in a haze of fear and anxiety. The demons inside my head seemed real and I was running from my own fear. I always saw myself as a little girl running through a field with something chasing behind me, so I kept running for most of my life.

What was I running from? Myself! The shadow that followed me didn't feel like it was part of me but a constant reminder of the dark side within all of us. Some days, the dark side took over everything else and there was no light to be seen or felt. In ways it was a safe place as I couldn't see what was coming for me. It is almost easier to sit in the dark than to reach out for the light. When we come out of the darkness our whole self is revealed and we may not like what we see or feel.

For me, the fear of seeing myself as I truly was became a block in facing my fears real and believed. To everyone else I was just an ordinary girl, but in my mind I lived many different variations of life. I lived with my family, I lived in my dreams, I lived in my fear, I lived a life that no one else could ever understand because I didn't understand it. I felt as if I could be all parts of me in different places at different times but not fully living in any of them. It was a way to escape myself and all the parts that I couldn't deal with at the time. In explaining this to you, it may read as if I was totally psychotic but, in fact, I was very together in a masked frail sort of way. I had learned to play the game of life and show the face that was needed in each situation. To me it was loading a programme into my mind that I would use in that day or that moment, files could be replaced with just a thought and I would become who I needed to be.

I saw myself like a robot at times, just functioning on demand but without the emotional attachment. I could carry out any task without anyone being aware of the underlying imbalance in my emotional or mental state. It was invisible armour that I had placed within my mind and it guarded my emotions from ever being revealed, and if they were I would surely explode into a million different parts and no one would ever be able to put them back together again. Of course, you can only run on automatic for so long until the day comes when you start to break down and slowly your inbuilt defences start to get slower until you no longer operate anymore. That is when you fall and that is, hopefully, when you learn you can get back up again. My aim is to reassure every person that no matter what you go through in life, you too, can help yourself to heal.

Ultimately, we are all just ordinary people living our day-to-day lives. Some of us overcoming extraordinary challenges and don't go on to write about them. I felt a strong desire to share in how from my lowest point in life, my most vulnerable place, how we all have an incredible inner strength, a resilience that pushes us to thrive. I want you to believe that you too have the same strength of mind, body and spirit.

In my life I have found many people that have guided and helped me through some of my struggles and learning, but I had to find my own way in learning what would work best for me. It is not always easy, but in doing so, you create the life you truly want for yourself. You take responsibility for how it all turns out. How your life turns out.

Through my own personal journey, I have battled with anxiety, depression, suicidal thoughts and a lack of understanding of what all of these labels meant to me. The shadows that I ran from were deep within my core and no matter how fast I tried to run they would invariably follow. No one in the world can fully understand what goes on inside your mind, only you can truly know that for yourself. Once we find a deepened understanding of the way we think, feel and engage with the world we can work towards identifying our individual needs and how to cope or deal with our daily challenges.

I do not claim to be a 'great writer' or philosopher. I don't claim to know all the answers to life's questions, but I can only share what I have learned along my path. In doing so, I hope that you, too, will find peace and acceptance in your life to go on to achieve what your heart desires. I have learned that we all need help at certain points in our lives and it is okay to reach out. I am reaching out to you in this book, please never feel like you are alone or walking your path in solitude. In truth, none of us are. We are surrounded by Divine love; it never diminishes, never fades and is available to each of us at all times. This is something I learned to understand more and more as my life progressed.

When we judge ourselves by how society sees us, we can sometimes feel threatened or pushed into labelling ourselves to fit in. I love the uniqueness of each and every person, personality traits and quirky ways are what make each of us stand out from everyone else. This uniqueness should be celebrated and encouraged in you and everyone you love.

In the end, all that really matters is that you love and accept yourself for who you are in each moment. In doing so you will find the strength to live another day and who knows, some day you may look back and see how far you have come and be amazed. Never give up on you.

Love Sharon

DARK NIGHT OF MY SOUL

"*Someone please help me.*" Those were the words that I screamed inside my head as I rolled on the floor of my rented box room in Galway city. Even in my desperation and darkness I still could not physically call out for help. I still hid my fear and shame from everyone around me. Who would understand and who could really help me? I just wanted the pain and hurt to go away. I just wanted it all to end.

I had just split up from a six year relationship and honestly felt whom could I turn to for help? I had lived my life robotically for 23 long years and I was ready to break down and not worry if I couldn't be put back together again. I was sick fighting. I had felt that I was on a secret mission all through my life and that someday someone would pop up and tell me you have succeeded in your training and passed the test. I had believed somewhere deep down that I was being watched and guided, the eyes that followed me in the shadows were somehow real and would one day appear just when I needed them most.

I looked out the two storey window of my little box room in a rented house in the city, and thought to myself "*If I ended it all, would it hurt any more than it does already, would anyone really miss me!*" In that moment, I felt completely alone and the screaming got louder in my head and from the deepest part of my soul. My heart ached so much that it felt like it was bursting out of my chest. I just wanted it all to stop.

I looked around my small room with a single bed, a chest of drawers and some old photos stuck to the wall, and thought to myself, was this it? Will this be my legacy to the world once I am gone? What lasting impression would I leave behind me? Was everything that I had ever endured just been a cruel twist of fate and there was nothing left to show for it. Sure, my family and friends would cry at my funeral and then just get on with their lives. Would they have remembered anything special about me or only talk of me on my anniversary? Did I really add anything to anyone else's life when I couldn't find one reason to believe I added value to this life?

It was sheer desolation and a darkness that even I could not sit in any longer. It felt heavy on my mind and my body and this time my heart could no longer hold its weight. I truly felt like I was being taken over from the inside out and if it continued there would be no trace of me, only a black shadow on the floor. I was disappearing and any little part of me that I had tried to create over the years was now dwindling from sight. I felt like I had been leaving my body little by little for many years and the last little bit that remained was now not able to carry the pain any longer, it had to escape.

My last memory was of pain, anguish, fear and loneliness as I lay on the floor. The slight rocking of my body curled up in the foetal position on a dusty old mat was the only sound in the room, my internal screams echoed in my mind and the tears that fell from my eyes felt like acid drops sitting on my face, they burned as a reminder that even crying did not release any of what I felt in that moment. It was like being tortured without any chance of being rescued and inevitably death would be a peaceful release. Time stood still in these moments of remembering and I was in and out of conscious awareness as if my mind had begun to shut down just so I would not have to process the million thoughts and feelings that had decided to resurface.

I began to fade deeper and deeper into the black hole of my mind, my body falling with it and eating me up, I was disappearing little by little. There were only the invisible eyes in the darkness and I screamed from my soul again *"Someone please help me."*

The next morning I awoke in my bed tucked in safely. Confusion, pain, aching, eyes burning, what had happened? Was I still alive? Did one of my house- mates come in and find me a desperate wreck on the floor and put me to bed? I checked the door, it was still locked from the inside, *"God, maybe I am going crazy?"* I couldn't even remember putting myself to bed! I just was so confused, as I looked around realising I was still in my little box room, nothing about it had changed but I had, a sudden calmness flowed through me. I was still alive.

Without realising it at that very moment, I had been saved. I was not meant to leave this life at that particular moment, I had been helped but not by any physical person. I had been spoken to and helped and it was *my* decision, *my* free will to stay on this Earth and make it the best life I possibly could.

I didn't realise I had a soul plan for 'Sharon.' I didn't understand back then that everything I had ever been through in my life had led me to that particular moment in my life where I questioned the purpose of it all. If it really was worth living. If life held any meaning for me, I knew it could make a difference to others. Without realising it I began a quest, a quest for life. I never knew it would lead me to this moment where I now sit and write these words I now share with you.

At times I felt great resistance to sharing my story with anyone, even writing the words brought up huge pain and sadness for me but also a freedom to express what I had kept inside for so long. We fool ourselves by believing we have dealt with everything in the past, it just can't be talked out of us, or masked by prescription drugs. It is part of who we are made up of, it is up to us how we choose to see it and feel it from this moment on.

I will tell you of how without even realising it or understanding it, I have always been helped, always been guided and I am exactly where I should be right now. To get to where I am now I will tell you some of my story. I want you to understand where I am coming from and how I got to this very moment where I decided to write the words that could help someone else to find their own path of healing. I will tell you of my experiences as I saw and felt them as a child growing up and how I feel about them now. I am not that child or young woman anymore frightened and scared.

I now feel I am Divinely Guided and I give thanks every day for choosing to remain on this Earth to fulfil my Soul's plan. Imagine not being able to get up every morning and see the sky, to feel my breath, to hear the wind, to smell the grass, to walk on this Earth, just to be. I am. I will always be. I invite you now to come on my journey and hope in some small way it will open your heart just a little to the beauty of the Divine Energy that we all are.

CHAPTER 1

Acceptance was the Key to my Freedom

So how does one gain acceptance after the 'dark night of the soul'? That is something I have been working on since that faithful night and am still doing to this very day.

There is no magic key that presents itself to you at a time of crisis, no magic door that will open in front of you and allow you to walk through into the freedom you so yearn for, it is all within yourself.

My acceptance came in a moment of pure darkness but had yet to realise it. In surrendering all my pain and fear in that moment of solitude, fear and isolation, I was no longer able to feel that there was a place for me in this world, so I let go.

I let go of all the pain that I had buried deep inside for 23 years, still too young to realise that this could be part of many other people's lives too. In my despair, I believed I was the only person ever to suffer in silence and that no one could help me find a way out of the torture that cast shadows in my mind, body and soul.

At that moment I felt the heaviness implode inside of my very being, for once I did not care if I lived or died. I just wanted all the pain to go away, to be free, even if I had no idea what that freedom would mean, leaving this Earth was my only option and I failed to even succeed at that.

From falling into despair and waking the next morning to find myself in the bed, tucked up safe and secure, a sudden wave of relief came over me. Then a sense of panic, what do I do next? I knew somewhere deep inside of me that there was a reason I was still alive and that maybe my time to start really living would begin from that very moment.

I can tell you that I did not jump out of the bed and start shouting from the rooftops *"I'm alive, I'm alive."* No. I kept the details of this night to myself for a very long time. I didn't feel elation at still being here; instead I felt trepidation, fear and a lot of anxiety. What now?

From that morning, I made up my mind that I would take it one hour at a time, one day at a time as this was the easiest way for my mind to focus on coping with living. If I were to think too far ahead, I would create more insecurity about my future self.

So that is exactly what I did. I started that day with an acceptance within myself that I only had to get through the next hour and when that hour was over, I got through the next hour and eventually I had a whole day done. I got through many hours in this way without feeling like I was going into a state of panic.

I started each day the same way, allowing myself to accept that I only had this day to get through and to make it the best possible day I could. In a way, it was a truly learning experience in being mindful and living in the moment, I did not even realise I was practising mindfulness, for me it was a coping mechanism that I now know brought many benefits to me throughout my whole life and still is.

As I worked my way through life, I was allowing myself to accept myself in each moment, it became a little easier to accept that I was no longer living in the past and was now truly in the moment, of course there were times when I would run away with myself and wonder what I would be doing in the future, this brought about a lot of anxiety as I could only see myself failing and having nothing to show for surviving the dark night of my soul, so I persevered with the living of day to day and trying not to think too much of the past, or of the future.

Acceptance really began when I started to allow myself to be who I was in each moment. I had always defined myself by my family and friends, the choices I had made and the mistakes I made with no sense of purpose. I floated along with life carried by the waves of other people's choices. When I was a child and even into early adolescents and adulthood, I was shaped by my conditioning and the thought patterns that had been taught to me from the people I was closest to and learned from. They only passed on the knowledge and understanding they had at the time. I could not change my past, it was part of me and engrained into my very DNA. Or could I?

This is something I began to realise as I accepted myself each and every day. I realised that my life to that point was a result of other people shaping my belief systems and not having to truly think for myself. In a way, it was easier to blame everyone else for the troubles I faced in my life and not to take responsibility for any part I may have played in it. I realised that I was still to a point, living in the past, in my thoughts and my feelings. I had trapped myself there. There was nobody else to blame as it was just me now and I wasn't being caged and fed the insecurities by anyone else, I was feeding myself with the old hurts and pains every time I felt sad or lonely.

I had to accept that being sexually abused as a child, was the result of someone else's choices. I had to accept the fact that abuse was about having control and power over the vulnerable and I had an abundance of vulnerability. I was only a child and what was happening to me, even if I didn't understand what it was called at the time, did not feel right. When feeling like you were a target for someone else's pleasure no matter how you felt about it, was having a deep psychological effect on my mental and emotional wellbeing. It taught me to mistrust and to hide my feelings. It taught me to grow up faster than any child should ever have to grow up. That innocence was not a given and can be taken away from you in any moment. Going from day to day with the fear that it would happen again and I could do nothing to stop it. Not being able to speak up for myself or explain to another human being what was happening to me. I had to accept that I did nothing wrong, that the shame I carried heavy in my heart was not mine, that the fear of being intimate as a young adult was as a result of someone else betraying my trust and invading my personal and very private space as a child.

I had learned to mentally and emotionally leave my physical body as it was happening. I didn't know this at the time, but in part of my own healing later on in life. I realised that it was a coping mechanism that I created as a child unable to cope with what was happening in that moment.

I can still picture myself as a child watching myself being abused and not having any attachment to the image. I didn't have the same detachment when it came to the fear or anticipation of the abuse reoccurring or to how I would learn to deal with the repressed emotions held within my cell memories years later.

Through my very early years, I also began to experience very lucid dreams and also visions outside of my mind. As a child I was terrified of these experiences as we had only heard of ghosts and vampires appearing at night and that they were coming to get you. I cowered under my bedclothes at night, begging myself to go to sleep and not to look out into the dark to see the faces that so often frequented my little bedroom or outside my window as if trying to get in. This was the start of my connection to Spirit world, to the ones that have passed from this earthly world and for some reason I was able to see them.

Most of these experiences happened at night and to an adult they would explain it by saying you were dreaming, and that children can imagine anything when they are afraid, I absolutely agree. It is something that we all do without realising it. We put an image with our fear based thoughts and allow them to grow into something that we believe is real.

I saw faces of people, not in physical form like you or I, but like a hologram of a person with expressions of sadness, smiles and some asking me to help them. I only recognise this now as an adult, as a child I believed they were going to hurt me. I experienced energy moving through and around me and again as a child I could not explain or understand what this was, so I imagined it as a large bale of hay and to control it I could make it grow smaller to stop the intensity of the feeling. My only respite was in my dreams, I loved going to bed so I could dream. I could go anywhere in my dreams and be as free as I wanted.

Most of my dreams were carefree and fun, there were no monsters, no one to harm me, no one to fear and everyone seemed to love everyone else with an acceptance that we are all equal. It was where I wanted to live all the time, but when I awoke I realised I lived in a different reality but no one could take my dream world away from me, it was my secret escape. Only in my dreams could I be really happy and loved unconditionally.

With all of these occurrences another experience was of someone – not physical, but one of my hologram people twirling my hair at night, this happened long into my adult life, but again as a child I was terrified it was another monster trying to eat me. I somehow sensed the person was there to help me, but being so afraid I never thought of asking the person who they were and why they were here, this is something I only learned to do many years later. I learned since, that this was my maternal Grandmother who had passed when I was only a toddler. As I learned to hide my emotions more carefully growing up, I also blocked these experiences from my mind as if pretending they were not really happening, I couldn't comprehend in my young mind, why I was seeing and hearing things that no one else appeared to speak about.

As a child I had heard many conversations and as with all children we are like sponges, we soak up information around us and take it as truth. How would we know any different, we are a product of our environment. Growing up, I believed that the way I grew up was pretty much how every other family in Ireland grew up too, we didn't have loads of money, but appreciated what we did have.

There was a lot of turbulence in our family life and I grew up being fearful of not having enough of anything, it was engrained into my psyche and I held it as a belief right up to much of my young adult life. When I started working part-time whilst going to school, my first wage packet was given to me in a small brown envelope with my name on it. I stared at it for ages, holding it in my young hands with the excitement of knowing that I had earned this, it was overwhelming, it was like I had won the lottery, it was all mine. For me that was when I started to realise that if you want something more you have to go out and earn it. It was one of my greatest lessons. I wasn't afraid of hard work and long hours, I would work any amount of hours and know the end result would be recognition of my hard work, this I know does not always come in monetary value, but in recognising that you had to put the effort in and would be rewarded for your dedication. It may not have always worked to my advantage financially, but there was a deeper meaning for me. I knew that to get anywhere in my own life, I was going to have to work that little bit harder.

I can't remember much of my school days from an early age, only that I had changed schools three times up to the age of eleven due to my family relocating as a result of my Father's work. Moving into a new home and entering a class that was already established was always hard, leaving friends behind for me was tough. I wasn't the most outgoing of children when I was younger and found it hard to feel comfortable in myself with new people. We all know that children can be particularly cruel, even if unintentional and it hit me hard to be called a 'blow in,' I wasn't even sure what that meant at the time, but I took it personally. I was right in the centre of their attention and I just wanted to be invisible and blend into the background. Sometimes we stand out for all the wrong reasons.

When I entered Secondary school, I thought this was the start of a whole new world, a chance to develop and grow with so many new experiences. New teachers, new subjects and new people that each were going to enhance my life in some way. I wasn't the best of students as I was easily distracted and liked to day dream whilst in the middle of a class. I loved a good joke and could sometimes be the clown of the class, I suppose it was a way of drawing attention to myself before they realised I wasn't really that confident or that as hard and all as I worked, I may never be an A student. I did spend a few classes outside the door for talking or laughing in class, I was always the one to get caught, even if I hadn't initiated the disturbance in the first place.

I loved English class where we were to draw from our imagination to write an essay or read a story which you could picture in your mind, including the characters and their surroundings. I loved how the story brought you on a rollercoaster of emotions whilst the story became alive in your mind. I got lost in these stories and for a little while escaped my mundane world. For the first two years of secondary school I was very diligent in my homework and took great pride in my copies being neat and tidy and getting approval from the teachers. In my third year, I discovered boys!

I don't believe I was anything special to look at in my teenage years, I had big blue eyes, short hair and a very big smile. I was friendly and wasn't short of a quick answer. That time, boys wouldn't usually ask you out themselves, they would get a friend to do it, so more often than not, a friend would say that *'such a fella likes you and wants to go out with you,'* I might say *"yes"* and then we would be boyfriend and girlfriend. Now the funny thing is, I often broke it off a few days later as I wouldn't have even had a chance to meet the boy in question and I think it was just the thrill of being admired by someone from afar. That, I suppose for me, was the start of realising that I wanted to be loved but also afraid to get too close to someone.

The first time that I really called someone my boyfriend and it really meant something was when I was fifteen. He was a few years older than me and I had seen him at a local disco, I was friends with his brother and had only heard of him but never actually saw him face to face. So when the opportunity arose to speak to him and he asked me to dance, I was totally in awe. He was attentive, talkative and always made me smile. His kisses were like something from the movies and I was falling in love with the idea of being in love. We never did anything more than kiss and cuddle, even though I know at one or two points there was an urge to go further, but I was so afraid of being that intimate with anyone, even with someone that showed me love in a way that I never knew before. I always told myself, firstly I was too young and secondly my Father would kill me if he found out! Plus the romantic in me believed that if a person really loves you, they will wait until you are both ready to take that next and very important step.

Now it wasn't all kisses and romance, we had out fights like any young couple and he didn't always understand my emotional needs, he had become part of my world and on looking back, he was probably the best first real boyfriend a girl could ever have. He taught me love is like a rollercoaster and learning to say goodbye was never easy. We went out together for two years at which time he was out of work and looking to immigrate to the UK. I was heartbroken. Someone who had become such a big part of my life was now going to leave, I started to feel very uncertain about life again.

Whilst I had been wrapped up in the haze of young love and floating through my life without a real thought for anything else, I had felt safe. I was now left with the realisation that without him I felt I had nothing, I felt empty. This I now know was how I coped with many things in life, I filled the void within myself with the love of another, with their hopes and dreams and put myself to the side. I had done this with my school work and focused only on the thought of meeting my boyfriend and how we were going to spend the weekend. I was truly a love sick teenager! So he leaves, I am devastated, I felt my heart was going to literally tear in half and I would never feel love like this again. I even told my Mother that when I finished school the following year, I was going to move to the UK to be with him. I was, after all, nearly seventeen! I was caught up in the romantic notion that love conquers all and never gave a thought to work, financial security or looking to what I really wanted for my own future. So for a long time after his departure, I got through each day with the hope and belief that we would be together again and everything would be perfect.

Back to the reality of school and now not having the distraction of my boyfriend, I realised that I was not doing well at my school work. I had lost interest in my studies and gave no thought as to this being my door to a future life that could bring many opportunities. I felt totally lost again. I know I tried, but trying to catch up on two year's work was not easy. I watched other classmates excel in the subjects we were learning and even planning what they were going to do at college, to me I went along with the excited conversations, but in my heart I knew I hadn't got a chance, I had missed my opportunity and had to accept that. But always a trier, I filled in the application form to attend college and believed somewhere deep inside of me that I might just have a chance. I am smiling now as I really was a dreamer, still am to be honest, but I believed that a miracle might occur and I would get really good exam results and be offered a place in college.

In the meantime, I had a call from a boy that had seen me in the paper for a function I had attended. He had managed to source my phone number and bravely phoned me to ask me out, I was shocked but also a little intrigued. He again was older than me and finished school, he drove his Father's car and was even working. I wasn't sure about meeting him as I was still in contact with my boyfriend in the UK and felt like I was being disloyal. So, like the good girl that I am, I wrote to my old boyfriend in the UK and told him that this new fella had called me to meet up, he was so kind and sincere and told me to go ahead and meet the new lad, as he didn't want me to stop living my life because of the choice that he made in leaving. He told me he would always love me and that if we were meant to be together some day, we would.

I took this as a sign and decided I would meet the new fella. Well, it didn't take long for me to decide, I started going out with the new fella and we spent a lot of time together getting to know each other and now that I was a little bit older and in my eyes a little bit more experienced in relationships, I could deal with being closer to someone this time. I was still at school and my fears of not keeping up with my school work went out the window once again. I was once again floating in the cloud of love and my feet were nowhere near the ground. I had allowed myself to become once again lost in emotional support from another and feel safe in the belief that they would make everything alright.

The day came for our results to be received and I opened mine with a little hesitation as I knew deep down that mine were not going to show what I wanted because I hadn't put in the effort or the work. So, opening the envelope I closed my eyes and when I opened them again, I realised that I had not passed all my subjects. I had done well in a few of them even surprising myself a little, but I still didn't have enough points to be accepted onto any course, I felt very sad but what I felt most was a disappointment in myself, I was the only one responsible for my results and I had to now accept it.

You move on, there was no time sit back and wait for an opportunity to come knocking at the door or your parents to fix it for you, I had to figure out what I was going to do next. At this stage I was a year going out with my new boyfriend and things had become quite serious in a short space of time and we were becoming closer in many ways. He had asked me to move in with him and I was over the moon, I was finally going to be a grown up and make my own choices. So we did exactly that, we found a flat and moved in together, I was seventeen. My Mother had not wanted me to move away from home at such a young age but again I didn't listen. I was free!

I started a full-time business secretarial course in our local town and as I was now living in the city, I had to commute every day for my course. I was also working part time in a department store and this helped fund my travel, rent and food, there wasn't much else left after that.

In the middle of all this, I became pregnant, I was still only seventeen. You would think I was old enough to know better, but I wasn't. The first thing that went through my mind was that my parents would go mad and I was absolutely petrified. Growing up in the 1980's doesn't seem like that long ago but it was still taboo to be pregnant out of wedlock. I felt the shame burning through my body and what other people would think of me, again I felt disappointed in myself. My boyfriend and I both inexperienced at real life and terrified with the idea of telling people, worried about how we would raise a child, we decided we would travel by ferry to the UK and have a termination.

This was one of the scariest times of my life, not knowing where we were going. Never being out of the country before, everything seemed like a huge task whilst dealing with the knowledge that I was pregnant at seventeen and in a few hours I would no longer be. We had no idea where to start, so we looked up a phone book for 'Abortion clinics' and we found one that was a tube ride away and made an appointment to see the counsellor who would determine if I was a suitable candidate for this procedure. All of this was done within a few hours of getting off the ferry and making our way to London on the bus. There was no time to see the sights or take a leisurely walk around like most young people that would come to visit a new city for the first time. We were on a mission and it was our job to get it done as quickly as possible. We needed to get rid of this problem and that is all we were focused on.

We sat in the waiting room of the clinic and I looked around at young girls and some older women all awaiting the same fate. I felt ashamed and embarrassed sitting there even though they didn't know me, they all knew I was there for the same reason they were and it didn't help. We were each alone in our own desperation.

Once my turn came I was promptly shown into the consulting room and asked to fill out a form. My boyfriend was told to remain outside as one of the questions on the form is are you doing this of your own free will. It was only then did I stop and think, am I? From the moment I found out I was pregnant, the only solution was how to get rid of the problem and not about how I felt or if I wanted to keep the baby. I felt helpless once again and cried my eyes out. I told the counsellor that I was terrified and it would not be taken lightly at home in Ireland, she understood and advised me of the details of the upcoming procedure, I realised that this meant it was definitely going ahead. Out I go with my completed form and was directed into the main clinic to prepare for the surgery. I was like someone lost in a fog only looking for the next step to take so that I wouldn't trip and fall.

As I lay in the cold and sterile theatre and they counted me down to sleep, a little voice inside me said *"please stop, I don't want to do this anymore,"* but again no words were spoken out loud. I went to sleep with tears rolling down the sides of my face. I awoke in a ward with women either side of me, curtains half drawn between beds and the only noise was of sobbing women and nurses trying to console them. I was still very groggy and tried to get my bearings, asking myself if it was over and what would I do now. I, too, cried but not in a loud sobbing cry. I cried silently for the baby I had terminated, for myself and for all the other girls that had to make that decision too. I cried for many things that had led me to this very point and wondered if you could ever truly recover from your past. I cried alone. I just cried.

On returning home to Ireland from the UK, I had to pretend we had a fabulous trip and it was a lovely surprise gift for my upcoming 18th birthday. Inside I was devastated. I was still bleeding from the procedure and felt like my insides had been ripped out. Of course, they hadn't, but it was the emptiness that left me feeling torn apart. There was no one to speak to about the experience and it was once again like everything else in my life, buried deep inside to fester and rot. My boyfriend and I got on with living life as normal and never really spoke of that ordeal. It was better left unspoken as we were both too young to truly understand the emotional implication it actually had on us or our relationship. I went on to marry this man after five years together and our relationship had many challenges. I had finished my course and worked in retail for the next few years. Life seemed to just go by without having to truly deal with any of the issues that were slowly burning up inside of me.

I was married for one year and our anniversary marked a decision to go our separate ways. I had come into the relationship as a child and was leaving an adult. We both had issues that we needed to resolve within our own lives which challenged our relationship and created more issues that I felt we were unequipped to cope with. As I look back now, it was a pinnacle moment in my life, without realising it I had come to a decision that was going to change the direction of my life immensely. I was 23 years old and I had nothing to show for it, in my mind I was a failure.

Walking away from what is not good for you seems easy, but sometimes it is easier to stay in that familiar place, even if you know it is not right for you. So I faced a future of uncertainty and I was on my own. It led me to a point in my life where I could no longer hide the feelings and thoughts I was having and they started to overwhelm me in my everyday life. I was scared frightened and totally isolated within myself, there was no way out and couldn't handle the pain of it anymore. It led me to that faithful night where I believed my whole world had fallen apart and I was about to break into a million pieces and never wanted to be put back together again. As I didn't succeed in that task, I now faced my biggest challenge – living!

I yearned for love and affection but was afraid of getting hurt or being used. I was allowing myself to truly be honest and open about who I was, who I am now and who I wanted to be. This was going to be the hardest part of my life.

Acceptance was knowing that I ran from my young life into an adult life where I believed I could escape and start a new life by running in to the arms of another and that they would save me. When we run from anything we are constantly looking over our shoulders afraid the past will catch up with us, but it didn't have to catch up with me before that faithful night, I had carried it around with me for 23 years like the martyrs of old, this was my cushioning, I had a reason to be the way I was and that was my great excuse for not fully living for many years.

Acceptance truly hit me when I allowed myself to not be defined by my past and live for who I was in each day. I would promise myself to be kinder to me and everyone that would cross my path from that moment.

I had to accept that my past life did not define me but had brought me to this very moment. I still didn't want to keep reliving it my mind over and over again. It was exhausting and sometimes even bored me. Could I not have new thoughts? In a way the discussion in my mind was the start of me learning how to trust myself and my own inner guidance. As a child and teenager, I had spoken to myself quietly in the night and asked for God or someone 'out there' to help me. I prayed under the bed covers for someone to come and rescue me. I waited and waited for that someone to come and they never did, so I let go of the hope of ever being rescued by an outside source. I had to do this myself. Was I now learning how to do that?

This was the scary part. How could I trust myself. The choices that I had made in the past were not always the best, they got me what I needed or thought I wanted at the time. Now I had accepted that I was responsible for my own life, I had to really start thinking about what is best for me now, today, right here in this moment, it took patience and a great deal of determination to stick with accepting I was now the leader in my own life. There wouldn't be anyone else to fall back on or to blame when things went wrong, it was up to me to take hold of the reins and ride on into my future. It might be a rocky ride, but I was willing to try, I wanted now more than ever to be myself, who that was I didn't really know, but I was finding the courage to learn.

Yes it is okay for me to tell you that acceptance is the key to my freedom but does real freedom come from just saying words in your own head? At first, I only said the words, the constant affirming that I accepted myself as I was, led me to eventually start believing the mantra that had become part of my daily routine. I had to relearn how to observe my thoughts, not get attached to them as thoughts will always come and go and we just have to let them. We are constantly being bombarded with subliminal stimuli from outside sources without being even aware of it.

Every day, no matter how mindful you are, you are still listening subconsciously to advertisements, media reports, conversations at work or at home and taking all that outside information into the subconscious. We may not be part of each conversation, but there are points that you will resonate with whether negative or positive, and they will sit in the subconscious awaiting a time to appear in the conscious mind when you least expect them. They usually appear when you are feeling low and the only thoughts you will notice are the ones that make you feel worse about yourself and your life, it is in that moment of awareness that we make the switch, get attached or switch the thought. This was something I was learning to do more and more each day.

There is no easy road to acceptance, but I promised myself that I would at least try. Each day I gently spoke the words *"I love and accept myself deeply and completely,"* sometimes I believed it and other times I didn't, but they were words that helped me get through the toughest of mental torture that only I knew was going on. I compare it to a battle scene in your head, you have two sides- the negative and the positive. It is up to you in choosing which side you want to be on and each day accepting that in every battle there is a surrender so that peace can be achieved in your life.

CHAPTER 2

Being Yourself

You know when a person tells you to 'just be yourself' and 'you will be fine?' Well, when I was growing up that was not true. To be truly myself would mean revealing my darkest secrets and showing the world that I was scared, lacking in self-belief and afraid of my own shadow. I played many characters all through my life, each one depending on who I needed to be in different circumstances to survive emotionally and mentally. I was now still playing a character, but this time it was trying to fit into a role that suited me and to start living as the main character in my own life. I had to believe that I was now directing every scene of my life and how it would play out.

We grow up being labelled, sometimes not intentionally, but we all have labels that we identify ourselves by. That may be a relationship status, our family's circumstances, careers, jobs or our financial status. We introduce ourselves as someone's daughter, wife or mother and promptly identify ourselves by what we do. Is this to validate ourselves to others or to ourselves? I didn't believe I had a good enough 'label' and wasn't even sure if I wanted a label. Our circumstances do not define who we are in each moment, they only define what we do. For me, I didn't feel like I did much of anything and this is where my quest for living brought about a want in me to define who I am in my own life. How did I want to see myself and was I too going to define myself by a label. The old question of 'who am I' echoed in my heart every day.

On my own now, the future was uncertain, I had no real plan and I certainly wasn't scripting how the next few years were going to turn out. I was living every moment just to survive and the only planning I did was getting up in time for work and planning what to eat that day. I told no one of my mindful existence and wore the mask so well.

To my friends and family, I looked okay. I had told my family of my marriage break-up and that it was for the best, they understood and supported me. I was working in retail and living in the city, so everyone felt I was doing okay. It is amazing how others can perceive your life as okay when you can disguise your true self. I was going out at weekends with friends like I had not done since I went to my first youth discos. It seemed like a whole new world. I was now 24 years old but I felt like I was 90! It took me a little while to get back into the swing of being single, not that I ever really was and that hit a chord with me too. I had always relied on someone else to show me that I was loved and if someone else could love me, then maybe I was okay. For the first time I was learning to love myself.

Being single for me was fabulous and frightening all at the same time. I loved the fact that I could go out when I chose to, even at a minute's notice and not have to check with anyone to make sure it was okay. The frightening part was that I didn't want to open up to anyone romantically as I was still going through the pain of my breakup, even though I knew deep down that it was the best thing for me at the time. I know now that I was using it as an excuse. I was afraid anyone would get close enough to find out that I was a complete mess and they would run a million miles to escape having to deal with all my emotional needs. These are the thoughts that went through my head each day and I had to be the peace keeper of my mind, just observing them without getting too attached. I tried hard, but on occasion I lost the battle.

During this time I had met a lovely girl who was working with me whilst she was on holidays from college. She was a few years younger than me and loved going out dancing as much as me. She encouraged me to go out and enjoy myself. This included the nights that we were working early the next day. I loved the excitement of it all, but not always the lack of sleep! We often worked until 11pm and went straight to the nightclub next door afterwards.

We didn't have much money so one drink would last us the whole night as we were too busy out dancing on the floor and singing along to the DJ. I felt alive in those moments, to me dance was an expression of my soul and I could let loose on the dance floor. I didn't care what anyone else was doing or worrying about being seen in those moments, I was alive and every cell in my being glowed with life, if only we could dance our way through life. I was starting to believe that I was okay and this was being reinforced by the many new people I was meeting along the way.

Time moved on and not having a relationship to fall back on, I started to see myself through my own eyes. Even though working and partying hard, I had time to spend on my own and reflect. I often sat in my little box room with no light on and watch the light that shone in from the street. It was a time I now know was like meditation for me, but again didn't call it that at the time. It was simply quiet time to reflect on how I was feeling, what thoughts I was thinking and giving myself the space to acknowledge and accept who I was in that moment. Sounds very deep for a 24 year old, but inside of me I felt a deep stirring as if something was coming and I had no idea what it was.

Apart from being afraid of what ever this was, I was also very excited. I felt reassured in those quiet moments and couldn't explain why. It started to bring up memories for me, as a child I used to keep a diary and I would write all my deepest fears and thoughts into a small copybook with pictures of pop stars on the cover. Often, I would scribble a boy's name enclosed in a heart shaped scribble, but the details I wrote inside the cover were not that of a love sick teenager but of a child that had a heavy heart and a mind filled with doubt and fear. I suddenly realised that it was my way of expressing my feelings and allowing them to be heard, by no one else only me, but at least I was letting them out. I felt a sense of relief at this thought, maybe I had let go more than I realised. When younger I had found an innocent way of coping with emotions I could simply not understand at the time by writing in my copybook, for me it was a way of expressing my feelings without being judged by others.

With this reflection time, it also brought up for me the memories of calling out to an unknown force, whether that was God or just anybody that would hear me roar from the silence of my heart. So, who was I speaking to and why did I feel like someone was listening? Was it a belief that I had been programmed into believing having been born into a Catholic family, or was it just an inner belief? I pondered this question quite a lot as a child and now it was back in my mind and being curious as I am, I thought about it from time to time. This led me to start telling myself that without anyone ever showing or telling me, I had found coping skills throughout my whole life and was still using some if not more of those skills to help myself now. The only difference now was that I was older and had a more inquisitive mind, I wanted to find out more about why people are the way they are and the best way to know this was to study myself.

Little by little, I started to believe in myself, I started to trust my gut feelings and instincts. I was asking myself the questions and without waiting for someone else to answer them for me, I was allowing the answers to come from within. It was starting to get very exciting. This curious journey not only brought about new ideas and inspirations but also I was starting to build my confidence and self-esteem. I had a long way to go, but I was slowly starting to find out who I was and believed that I had so much more to find out. I was now truly being myself, not for anyone else, but just for me. If I could be true to myself, then I could be true to everyone else. But first I had to find out what my truth actually was. I began to question my past beliefs and if they actually resonated with who I was now and who I wanted to become.

No one will believe in you if you do not believe in yourself. I wanted to believe in myself and I wanted others to believe in me too, I still had that niggling voice inside my head telling me that I wasn't good enough and it showed up when I was trying hard to show people who I really was, I think I tried too hard. People believe in you when you are happy and content in your own skin and not worry what others think of you. I was still looking for the approval of others and deep down I knew I wanted to be loved and accepted for me, but first I had to start with loving and accepting myself, not just when I was alone in the dark, but also in the bright light of day unafraid to be seen or noticed, flaws and all. Being myself, felt like standing naked in the middle of a concert and the spotlight shone directly upon me for everyone to see. Of course, they only see the naked physical body and don't know what lies beneath the surface, but most people judge by first impressions. I wanted people's first impression to be one that was believable by me and by them.

The hardest part of being myself was with the people who knew me before this, for them they had seen the outward changes in my life but as of yet, I wasn't ready to let them know the inward changes. Life continued as normal for them and I was in the process of living my life in a whole new way, learning to live from the inside out, sounds crazy but that is the way I felt it was at the time, if I could get it right in my head, then it would be right in my reality. My dearest and closest friends were always there and to this day still are, for they believed in me even when I couldn't do it for myself. They accepted me for who I was and slowly they would accept the changes that I needed to make so that I could truly believe in the person I was and wanted to become.

Being *yourself* is truly about accepting every part of you, your life and all the mistakes you made along the way. It is also about recognising the achievements, no matter how small and focusing on what will bring the most joy into your life in each moment. For me, I started believing that life could offer us anything and it was up to us to accept it or reject it, now I had a choice. Life is happening for us not to us, being true to your heart brings about the greatest of changes in your life and in the lives of others.

Through all of my reflecting and quiet moments, I was starting to see the changes I was creating in my own life. I had taken my power back and allowed myself to paint the picture of the life that I wanted, I had a blank canvas each and every day and it was up to me to not paint by numbers and follow someone else's interpretation of what my life should look like. But, to create a whole new image in my mind first and then take the steps to bring it to life. I believed I could do it, one stroke at a time.

CHAPTER 3

Commitment

I laugh as I write this now, never the most committed person when I was younger, I suppose I was afraid of failing or most importantly of succeeding. I really wanted to be good at something, but up to that point, I didn't believe I really was. I remember being told that no matter what job interview I went for I would get it as I had a great personality and a way with people. This I took to heart and believed it, not just because somebody else told me, but because deep down I knew I was, and still am a people person.

From the moment I started working, I always treated everyone with the respect and kindness that we all deserve. It is just a pity that not everyone in the world thinks the same, but again we cannot judge another as we have no idea what is going on in their life at that time. My very first goal was to always treat people the way I would like to be treated. I have stuck with the formula all of my life, remember that old saying *"what you give out, you get back!"*

So what did I want out of life? That is the million dollar question for most people. I had watched other people with big dreams and ambitions through school years and as I got older, I admired them so much. They had a passion and a purpose to living their lives, they knew what they wanted and were doing everything in their power to go out and make it happen. How could I do this too? I can tell you that it took me many years to really figure it out, but I was learning as I went along. Two more great learning lessons were coming my way and it was time to step up to the mark. It is okay to sit back and contemplate life, but only when you start living it can you see the rewards of your efforts. Now it was time to put all of my accepting and believing in myself to the test, could I really commit to myself and live the life I so wanted. I still wasn't sure what it was but I had a deep burning in my gut to go out and live more.

Meeting John taught me valuable lessons. He was five years older than me and a friend of a friend. I had met him briefly a few times and, of course, I noticed how good looking he was, but most importantly there was something that

I felt was deeper than just his looks. He had an inner strength and kindness that shone through his eyes and his smile. When he spoke it was with a gentle ease that made me feel safe and comfortable in his presence. . It was still only 4 months since my marriage break up and I wasn't too sure about getting involved with anyone, so I went on a date with him to the cinema. To this day I couldn't tell you what we saw, I was so nervous, it was like being 17 all over again! There was a lovely connection between us and as grounded and all as John was, he was also nervous. This is where my lesson began. I was trying to live in the moment, but my fear and doubt started to return. Questions I went over and over in my head started to take over. John knew I was separated but in 1994 in Ireland there was still no divorce, so where would this relationship go? I realised more and more that my emotional turbulence was still very much bubbling away under the surface and it took this lovely man to show me that no matter how much love he was willing to give to me, I could not totally accept it as I still didn't believe I deserved it. So the easiest thing for me to do was to break up with him.

On looking back, I realise that I was so wrapped up in my own feelings, I didn't take John's into consideration. I made the excuse that it would be much simpler if we broke up as we could never get married anyway. John had told me in the first week of our relationship that he wanted to marry me and it frightened the life out of me. What I didn't understand was that John could see the real me, the *me* that loved life, the me that was a little sad inside but wanted to be as happy as I possibly could every day. He saw the part of me that wanted to reach out and hold him and tell him I would never let him go, but that is something I couldn't promise to him or to myself at that time. I used so many excuses for breaking if off with him but he always came back. He accepted and believed in me, even loving me more than I loved myself. It was the beginning of a love affair not only with John but with myself.

I remember writing a letter to someone over 20 years ago saying *"you can't help who you fall in love with,"* this is so true. Whether the experience will bring you joy or pain, it is part of your journey. The person you fall in love with is felt deep within your soul and you are attracted to the person that resonates with what you are vibrating on an energetic level, so without being aware of it, I was actually vibrating a beautiful frequency of love and bringing into my life the person that would show me who I was when unable to see it in myself. I tell people now that *'the teacher will show themselves to the student when they are ready,'* does not always mean in an academic way, it can be in the learning of the greatest life lesson of all – Love.

This is where I really started to commit to myself and to what I wanted. So, yes, we had a few blocks in our way, there was no divorce in Ireland, but as I had got married in a Catholic church, I could at least start the annulment process. I was also committing to John, even though he knew I loved him deeply, I wanted to show him that I was serious about our future, that I was making plans for a future where we could grow together. The process was long and difficult. I won't go into the details of the annulment process but after over four years we received a declaration to say the 'marriage' was null and void, basically that it never took place. Amazing how a part of your life can just be erased by an official stamp and a signed form. It was a great celebration for myself and John as this meant we were able to move on. Not long after that divorce came into Ireland and I was officially single - decreed by state and church, so with a deep breath and a very open heart I went forward into my new life with John. We were engaged and ready for the next chapter of our lives together and I was so committed in making this part of my life the happiest ever, again a commitment to myself in that I was allowing joy and love to be the foundation of my life going forward. If you build a solid foundation, it will stand the test of time, this goes for everything in your life. If you feel a burning passion deep inside of you and you can't wait to do it, it is right, but sometimes that passion is a little flame that you build up gently and easily until you are ready to let it burn bright.

As I had now made the commitment to John and myself in our relationship, I wanted to take it a step further and deal with the niggling issues of my past. I had heard someone speak of a counsellor in the city that dealt with marriage issues, so I made an appointment with her and in my head had everything I was going to say.

My anxiety levels started to rise again, what questions would this counsellor ask me and what was I prepared to tell her. There was a sudden panic in my head and I started to see images of her shocked face and utter disgust at my life, I started to believe the counsellor would condemn me for all my past actions and run me out of the therapy room. Of course, these fears were all unfounded. I met a lovely older lady at the door of the counselling centre and was greeted warmly and invited into a small room with two chairs and a little table. My heart was pounding and I was wearing the mask of control *"keep it together Sharon,"* I repeated over and over in my head. My body had gone into a fight or flight response and I wanted to run as fast as I could out of the room so I wouldn't have to deal with what I perceived as a threat – my memories! Her beautiful soft voice and warm energy, allowed me to calm down little by little, she didn't pressure me into speaking or answering questions immediately, but gently spoke about how she was there to help me in whatever way I felt I needed at that time. I took a few deep breaths and in my mind had the words to speak out loud but instead I burst into tears. I couldn't hold them any longer, I was terrified. This was the first outside that I was going to tell some of my story to and the child inside of me came bursting out with muffled tears and nearly went into convulsions. She gave me the space to do so.

What seemed like forever, was probably only about 10 minutes and I calmed down, wiped my face and nose and started to speak very quietly about why I believed I was there. I told her that I had split up from my husband and that I had now met John and wanted to commit myself to loving him and being loved. She didn't react, only gently smiled and told me how lovely it is to be loved by another, I thought about this for a moment and thought *"yes, it is lovely."*

So our little session began and I spoke about anything that came into my mind. It was probably a bit of a lucky dip as I had so much to talk about. She listened patiently and only reached out to hand me a tissue when I allowed the tears to flow. I realised from the session that all I ever really wanted was for someone to listen to my side of the story, the child's side, the teenager's side, the young adult's side and now it was my side to tell, a young woman with years of pain deeply locked inside unable to express it before now. I felt relieved and exhausted all at the same time. I had gone to counselling to try to deal with the many past issues that had deeply affected my life and to understand that my earlier traumatic childhood had influenced the choices I made as a teenager and young adult. To help me commit to my present relationship, I had to revisit my past to understand that it was okay to speak of the things that had happened to me as a child. Furthermore, that the choices I made as a teenager and young adult were a reflection of the emotional and mental awareness I had at that time.

I was committed to seeing the counsellor each week, I was reliving so many memories that I felt like I was back in that time when I spoke to her, at one point I returned to being a child and felt like crawling in under the little table and hiding, the fear was still inside of me and I had to love that little girl and tell her that she was now safe.

I promised my inner child that I would love her and protect her to the best of my ability and that she would always be listened to by me. I used to see her in my mind, a little blonde girl with a white nightdress standing barefoot with her hands clasped together, she looked lost and alone and barely a smile crossed her face when I first met her. This was the way I had felt inside for so many years and without realising it, had detached myself as an adult from those childhood fears that lay dormant in my emotional and mental body. I could no longer ignore this beautiful but very frightened part of me, I wanted to pick her up and hug her so tightly and tell her that everything would be alright now. I told her that I couldn't change anything that happened to her in the past but that she no longer needed to be afraid. I did this on many occasions and each time her image grew stronger, her eyes became brighter and her smile grew from the inside out. I was healing my inner child in order to heal my adult self, I realised that I had to go back in order to move on, a valuable lesson I have learned that has helped me even to this day in my own work.

In this time I had also changed my career options. I had left retail and now worked in a hotel. I loved the buzz of hotel life, people coming and going, conference, weddings, parties with many a celebrity passing through the doors. It was so glamorous from the outside looking in! This was going to be my second greatest lesson. When I interviewed for the position, I was one of a few hundred, there was a psychological assessment along with a medical and one to one interviews. My stomach jumped inside of me looking at all the other people, some with years and years of experience in hotels all over the world and here was little old me having come from a retail background, how did I have a chance!

But I did, my personality won through over my skills and maybe the need in me to prove that I could achieve anything that I set my mind to. At the first introductory meeting, one of the Managers in the hotel- a lady, stood up in front of us in a red and black dress, she looked so confident and spoke so well. I thought to myself, I want to be like her when I grow up. Not realising this woman would become my new boss and I would be working with her very closely for many hours and days to come, she would also become a lifelong friend. She taught me the many key skills of hotel business, I was respectful to staff and guests alike and was noted for always remembering their names and having a big smile on my face to greet them.

Over time, the hotel was often short staffed and during these times the pressure of work was fraught and difficult. It was a bit like 'Fawlty Towers' and you would laugh at the madness of it all. As I worked, I also noticed how other people were treated and especially those that were unable to stand up for themselves. It was one thing to be treated badly yourself, but to stand back and watch someone else being treated badly was unforgiveable. I am not sure where my courage or strength came from, but one day I found a way to stand up to those in authority and even though I shook in my shoes, I knew it was something I had to do.

In the hotel industry, the staff rely on guests' tips to make up a big part of their wages each month. Because I was always on front of house duty, I received many tips and some of them were very generous. It was the guests' way of saying thank you and that your efforts were appreciated. I always felt a great sense of appreciation when a guest left a tip. The staff tips were joined together and broken up evenly every month to be distributed, I am not sure when it started to become apparent, but we were not receiving our tips and certainly not all that we had genuinely earned from our efforts. I was very lucky in that I lived with a solicitor friend at the time and she wrote a letter on my behalf demanding our tips. I photocopied it many times and placed all over the hotel for other staff to read and there was an immediate reaction.

The staff were delighted but some of the management were none too pleased. I was called into the Manager's office and told that this was unacceptable and basically told I could be fired for such behaviour but I knew my rights and was not afraid. For the first time in my life, I felt like I had taken a stand to defend my rights and the rights of others that I respected. When you work hard, it is only right that you receive what is due to you. It taught me to speak up for myself and that your voice can only be heard if you speak the words that need to be spoken. If I had sat idly by and allowed this to happen, nothing would be done and we would have felt used and disgruntled silently, it would have caused more negativity within our hotel family and this would in turn affect our guests and their stay. I was called into a meeting with one of the Managers and given a warning about causing disruption in the running of the hotel. I aired my disgust at the way we were being treated and that we were entitled to our dues. I was told that our tips would be gathered until December and distributed evenly amongst the staff then. I knew it was just a ploy to keep me quiet and to pacify the rest of the staff.

If you do not deal with things as they happen, they fester and start to affect everyone around you. This is true in all areas of our lives. As a result of this intervention, I knew my time in the hotel was coming to an end. I could not work for people that did not respect their staff. I did not realise at the time I was being head hunted by an International Telecommunications Company who had frequented the hotel on many occasions to hold their staff training or conferences, I had made an impression and they wanted me to come and work for them now. You get back what you put out. I was over the moon. Suddenly, someone wanted me on the basis of my work ethic and personal interaction with their top level Managers and staff, I was going to work in a company that appreciated your efforts.

It is up to each of us to speak up for those that are unable to for whatever reasons. I had spent much of my life unable to voice my opinions or for what I knew to be wrong, but now I had a choice and I was airing my views loud and clear. It wasn't about being right all the time, but I was not going to have any regrets anymore. I was committing to the belief in myself and if I didn't take a stand, I would be letting myself down. By doing so, I moved from a place of fear into a place of power, not to have power over anyone else, but to stand firm in my truth. As I did this, it changed my vibration to a place of letting go and opened new doors to a life that I was creating and allowing to flow more freely. I had made a promise to myself that I was going to do my best each and every day. Sometimes, doing your best means having to stand up for yourself and others. I kept my promise. We got our tips in the December and I left the hotel.

CHAPTER 4

Drive to Succeed

A person with drive to succeed has goals and puts effort in to reach those goals. The drive to succeed takes persistence, effort and accomplishing what you set out to do, whether you set your own tasks or are given tasks by others. I wanted to succeed at all tasks and now realised that I was driven by a deeper source within myself to accomplish anything I set my mind to. For the first time in my life, I truly wanted to do something more. Opportunities had arisen in my personal and professional life and I was seizing every one of them. I might have felt nervous about moving forward but I turned it into a joyful excitement that motivated me in so many ways. This was a new alternative way of thinking for me as I only took it day by day for the past few years, but now I was starting to think about what I wanted to create in my life, where I wanted to go and what I wanted to do. It was like something had moved into my energy that was urging me to just not settle with what I believed life was giving me, I knew I was allowing life to be created by my enthusiasm and desires. It was very exciting and I was really starting to enjoy being alive.

I was now 26 years old and had started in my new job. We had people from all over the world visiting us, whether it be clients or colleagues from the American and Canadian office. I loved being in the buzz of it all and meeting so many new people, I was also learning about a new side of telecommunications and programming that I knew nothing about. No matter what you do or where you go in life, there is an opportunity to learn and grow. I wanted to learn more and within a year I was promoted to Project Administrator and worked alongside a wonderful VP over research and development. There was 140 plus people on our team and they were all amazing. I loved the daily interaction, the frequent visitors and plans for our team to travel to the now Canadian owned offices and also to see the new college graduates coming in to start their careers in their new working environment. There was never a dull moment for me, I was getting paid to be with people each and every day and I loved it.

My VP had great confidence in my ability and in my performance review he encouraged me to learn and continue my studies. I still keep in contact with him to this day and look at him as another role model in my life. He was firm, but always patient, kind and understanding. I admired him so much for all the work that he did in our office, but also having to travel so much with a young family was extremely hard. I don't think people realise that with a big title and a higher position in the company you really do have to put in more work and also oversee that your team and your product are all running in order. My lesson learned from him was - encourage others, see the best in yourself and others, be firm when needed but also remember that kindness is remembered.

I wasn't always the best employee as some of the work truly went over my head and I knew I really didn't want to work in the telecommunications industry forever, I just loved working with all the people and some I have still remained friends with. I had a drive inside of me but it wasn't in this work, I knew that, but of course couldn't figure out what it actually was. The more I tried to figure it out, the further away I got from the answer. I was trying to force it to come and nothing that is forced comes from a place of love. I loved people and working with them, that was enough of a purpose for me now. The name of the job was not that important but someone had believed in me and helped me to take a step up the ladder in my own self-belief and in building my self-confidence. I was starting to recognise that I was driven in many aspects of my life, driven to succeed in being me. It may take me a lot longer to finally figure out what I wanted to do, but in the meantime I did what I loved and that was working with people every day that appreciated my efforts and encouraged me to acknowledge my skills and abilities, no matter how big or small to help me to grow from there.

I think it was actually the first time that someone offered to help me progress in my working life, so to me it was them approving of me, something I had sought in my younger days but for different reasons. When you appreciate others, it encourages them to do better, not only for themselves but to show you that they respect your support. The greatest gift you can give to another is appreciation, something we all need to remember for ourselves and the people in our lives. We can put ourselves into boxes, whilst boxing other people in a category that suits our society, but in the end we are all human beings trying to do the best we can with what we have.

I now was ready to focus on the positive influences in my life and how I could show them my appreciation was investing in my future.

Driving a car was also a way of me taking control. I remember John telling me as he tutored me one evening in a quiet car park that *"the car does not control you, you are in control"* this really hit a chord with me. Without my input and interaction, the car would simply just stand still, it is the same as our lives, if we don't put in any effort to move, life continues around us and this is where we believe things are happening to us instead of for us. I wanted to learn to drive on the road so I could go more places and be more independent in my own life.

To me it was an analogy of life, don't just be a passenger and expect to be taken where you want to go. If you really want to have the freedom to go where you want to go, you must get in the driver's side and take control, watching all the road signs along the way so you don't get lost. You decide where you want to go next.

CHAPTER 5

Life & Death

I'm going to return back to family of origin for this chapter. My Family consisted of my Mother, Father and my five siblings when I was growing up. I was the middle child. In 2012, I found out we had a half-brother and Sister whom my Father had from a previous relationship before he met my Mother. I have had the honour of meeting my half-brother and his family and we have a really close connection even though we only met a few years ago, it is like we have known each other forever.

My Father had bouts of depression and was very erratic and I never felt I could rely on him in the way that I could with my Mother. We didn't have great financial stability but did the best we could. Life was happening to me then and not for me.

My older Sister had been born with severe disabilities and couldn't walk or talk. Back in 1970 the doctors didn't hold out much hope of her living as she had developed meningitis also. My Mother was told that my Sister would not survive. My mother refused to give up on her little daughter and believed that as long as she was breathing, there was a chance. To this day, my Mother has never given up on any of us, even my Father, as she has the biggest heart anyone could ever have.

My Sister did survive and my Mother was able to bring her little girl home. For most of my Sister's young life, my Mother had to care for her without specialist equipment, she just had her two arms, a strong back and a Mother's love.

As my Sister was getting older, it was getting harder for my Mother to lift her from bed to the chair, she was growing but needed the full time care and attention twenty four seven. A new specialist centre had opened up in the city for children with physical and mental disabilities. It was time for my Mother to release her loving hold by giving herself and my Sister the freedom they both needed, it was one of the hardest decisions my mother had to make in her life. My Sister would live there from Monday to Friday and receive physical therapy and do all sorts of exercises, crafts and therapies to improve her lifestyle, none of which my Mother would be able to do at home with five other children. It was a beautiful home away from home for my Sister, the carers and staff were all so kind. They spoke to my Sister like they would speak to any child.

Of course, my Mother was heartbroken. She knew this was the best thing for my Sister but a part of her felt like she was giving her child away, the centre was offering her specialised care but her heart must have ached when my Sister left the first time. The more my Mother saw my Sister in her new surroundings, the more she realised that it provided a better quality of life and my Sister was as well- loved as she was at home.

There are so many special children in the world, but my Sister was very special to us. She was the Angel in our house sat quietly in the corner of our lives in the midst of everything. When she smiled at you it was like a silent gift of love. We may not have ever truly 'known' our Sister or what her thoughts or feelings were, but the look she gave us was enough to know that she loved us. I truly believe that she was an Angel on this Earth, one here to help a family going through hard times to know that there was a shining light of love sitting in our front room.

A few months before my Sister passed, she became very unwell. She had lost a lot of weight and found it hard to breathe. We knew that her time was coming close to leaving us. I remember the day she passed, we had been into visit her and my Mother sat at her bedside. I asked my Mother to come home and have a rest that night as she was exhausted, she didn't want to leave but I believe somehow my Sister was only able to pass once my Mother was gone. She passed at 5.40am the next morning. We got the call and rushed to her side. She was so beautiful laying there so peaceful and truly looked like an Angel, still warm and looking like she was just asleep but we had lost her from this world and it was heart breaking to watch my Mother lose one of her children, especially this very special child.

The next few days were frantic organising the funeral, cleaning the house and all the time having to deal with grief. It is not something I had ever experienced in my life with someone so close to me. My Grandmother and

Uncle had passed away years before that but it never had this effect on me. I had lost someone not only close but also someone very special in my life. My Sister had never been able to speak to us and tell us how she was feeling. She was laid out in the coffin in our front room and I whispered in her ear to please come back and tell me some time. Little did I know that she would.

As I sit here and think of my older Sister who was a beacon of light for us whilst growing up, I also think of the many things she had missed out on, going to discos, having boyfriends and all the things that go with growing up, but that is just because I knew what those things were and my Sister was oblivious in her little world to what happened outside the door of our house or the house she lived in the city. The people that came to pay their respects to my Sister and our family on her passing were mesmerised by this beautiful girl lying in the coffin. Most people commented how beautiful she was and how angelic she looked. We had some very funny moments too, like when a neighbour of ours who would have known our family well, came to pay his respects, we had a photo of my Sister and a photo of the 'The Blessed Virgin' on a table beside the coffin, the neighbour leaned over and as he looked at the Blessed Virgin picture he said, *"isn't She beautiful in that photo,"* thinking this was a photo of my Sister when she was alive, it took everything for us not to laugh out loud, but we hadn't the heart to tell him he was looking at the wrong picture. I am sure my Sister was with us in Spirit and having a good laugh too.

My two little nieces were at the house that night and they weren't exactly sure what all the commotion was about. One of my nieces who was about five years old at the time seemed to stick by my Mother as if she could feel every bit of heartache my Mother was feeling at that time. My Mother tells the story of a locket she wore around her neck and as my niece and her were walking through the house, my little niece picked the head of a flower and placed it into my Mother's hand and said *"here Nanny, this is a flower to remember her."* My Mother placed that flower inside the locket and it remains there to this day. It was such a special moment to see a little child respond so lovingly to how an adult was feeling and to behave in a way that children commonly do, with unconditional love and kindness.

We knew this was the moment that we all had to say goodbye to seeing my Sister's physical being ever again, but nothing was as hard as seeing my Mother say goodbye. I had wondered what it might have been like to lose a parent when I was younger, but never imagined the pain a parent could feel losing a child of their own. We, as a family, held hands in the front room where her coffin lay and the priest read out the prayers. We muttered replies to the prayers as we held back the gulping tears. I looked at all the faces of my family and each one had pain etched on their faces, maybe it was just me but with my Sister's passing, it brought up many memories of the past - good and bad. It was a time to say goodbye to her and hold her memory in our hearts forever. We were all now adults, but in that moment of grief, we were all just children.

Whilst organising the funeral my Mother found the poem that she had written many years before. It is the most heartfelt poem I have ever read, and it shows that my Mother really believed my Sister was a very special gift and was only on loan to our family. The poem goes as follows;

God's prayer to the parents of a Special Child

God said *I give to you this child, for you to call your own.*

She needs love and understanding, and a good and happy home.

She won't grow up and leave you, like the others do, but will bring you peace and happiness, that's given to a few.

Sometimes you'll feel that you can't cope and you can't take it anymore, and the sadness deep inside you, will cut you to the core.

Remember I am with her and always with you too.

I bring a blessing to this house when I give this child to you.

In her family, this child will have her place, you will see the look of gratitude each day upon her face.

She'll have a family who love her, and with her would not part, they'll remember her with love, forever in their hearts.

Maybe in a few years I will come and take her home, but don't be sad and lonely, you won't ever be alone.

She'll be always watching over you, with you her love will stay, till you meet again in heaven on that grand and happy day.

I read this poem out at my Sister's funeral mass and tried hard to hold back the tears. My Mother's words were also a special message to every parent in that church, our children are only on loan to us and we should cherish each and every minute with them.

We buried my Sister that afternoon. She was 28 years old.

With her passing, I started to question my existence, why we came here and what our purpose was. What was the purpose of my Sister's existence, bound to a body that within held a soul so pure and wise, unable to express with words what she thought, felt or heard? Was there a purpose?

This questioning went on in my mind for a long time as I dealt with the grief in my own way. There is no rule to how one should grieve the loss of a loved one. It is a personal experience that we must all go through. In our grief we realise the deep love we shared with that person, how losing them in our physical lives, leaves a gap that we are sometimes unable to fill. It is a journey that we are inevitably going to face in our lifetime and there is no preparation. For me, it was another part of my life that brought me closer to understanding love and accepting that the people we love won't always be there to touch, hug or talk to, but I was soon to learn that their existence is not just in the physical and we are never separated, even by physical death. My Sister, although passed from this world, would be my teacher in this lesson.

CHAPTER 6

Angels in my Life

When I got pregnant at 17 I was young, immature and fearful of what other people would say and how I would cope as a young mother. This time, eleven years later, there was no fear. I was 28 and pregnant.

I felt a great love for this new life inside of me. I sat on John's knee and said if it is a boy we will call him 'Matthew,' and I was so very happy at that very moment. I was totally secure in myself with John and this new baby on the way. I had never really felt that in my life before and it was the best feeling in the world. Yes, John and I were having a baby! I was nervous of being a mother but somehow I felt this little soul was coming to help me, to show us the unconditional love between a child and a parent and because he had chosen us above anyone else to be his mammy and daddy.

Matthew was born on the 30th January 2000. It was the most harrowing physical experience I ever went through but it was even worse watching John standing by my side feeling helpless. He was my rock and as long as I could see his face I knew everything would be alright. Matthew must have loved me so much as it took him three days to be delivered. On the third day I heard the nurses speak of a 'C- section' and I thought to myself *"please God help me get this baby out, I can't let him go through anymore"* and so I pushed with every last bit of energy I had and our little boy was born, 7 lbs 2ozs. My God, the love that I felt for that little baby was immense. It was like he had always been part of our lives and it was hard to remember what did I ever do before he came along. He truly was our blessing. Yes we had to get up and do the night feeds, we were sleep deprived, our freedom was halted and it was a major adjustment in our lives, I was exhausted but I wouldn't have changed it.

John had to return to work, it was very strange being at home with a new baby by myself and with no adult contact all through the day. Unless of course family or friends came to visit. I did feel isolated and a little bit out of my depth, but I got through it and Matthew grew into our lives.

I watched this little baby sleep and grow each and every day. His little smile could melt the toughest heart. To think he grew inside of me and now was a fully formed little person lying asleep in my arms. When he looked up at me it was like there was nothing else that mattered in that very moment. It was another love I had never experienced and it was truly amazing.

As we had already planned the wedding before I found out I was pregnant, we decided to keep the arrangements and marry that April. In my wisdom I thought that three months would be enough time to lose the baby weight and be back to my size 8. How wrong I was!

All of the normal wedding preparations were done already but I still had no dress, being a bit of a rebel, I wanted to wear red, so I got the material and a friend of my Sister's made the dress and was also going to make the flower girls dresses. I left it with her and continued being a new mom. I really didn't think too much about what I would look like and was just waiting to be married to John and have everyone celebrate with us.

I went for fittings for the dress and it all seemed great, the flower girls dresses weren't started but I trusted that all would work out for the day. So, when it came to our wedding day, not only having to get myself ready and beautified, I had a little 3 month old baby to wash, feed and dress and hope that he didn't puke up before the church. I got my dress and as I look back now I didn't give much thought to it or myself. My Sister went to collect the flower girl dresses and she phoned me to say they weren't even finished, there was panic, my Sister ended up sewing the sleeves together and just hoped they wouldn't fall apart walking up the aisle. I am an organised person and am always on time so this was madness for me. I couldn't wait to walk up the aisle and see John but I had to wait for the flower girls. We eventually got to the church an hour later than we should have been there. You just look back and laugh now as there is always a funny side to every story.

I didn't have the best relationship with my Father, but he did walk me down the aisle as it *'wouldn't look right if he didn't.'* My family and friends all gathered around us on this day to celebrate with us. Myself and John made our speeches and thanked everyone for coming. When I gave my speech I thanked John for being in my life and that Matthew and him made me feel complete. I really was so ecstatically happy at that moment that nothing else mattered, past or future. I still think of our first dance at the wedding and tears flowed down my face. The realisation that I deserved love and I felt at home in it. I was in love with life.

John, Matthew and I continued living in the city and we had planned to build a house near my Mother in the country. The house seemed to take forever to build and we had to pull all our funds together and start thinking of paying a mortgage, something neither of us had ever done before. We got another lovely surprise in that our daughter 'Alannah' was born 21 months after Matthew. I knew it was going to be a girl and had her name picked out already. I remember my paternal Grandmother saying '*a leanbh*', was an Irish word for child, I thought to myself years ago if I ever had a little girl I would call her Alannah, not knowing if the name existed or not, when I became pregnant with her it seemed the only name that fit her. So, like the ball of lightning that she is, I went into labour at home and tried to stay there for as long as possible. I felt okay about rolling around the sitting room floor of my house and running to the bathroom when I felt like I was going to throw up.

I had gone to the hospital around midnight and I wasn't even dilated 1cm so I asked if I could go home as I was only a 10 minute drive away and would return if the pain got unbearable. I wasn't in my bed 5 minutes when the pain got unbearable so I continued downstairs breathing through the pain, John and Matthew were fast asleep and my mother was staying over to mind Matthew. She came down about 5am and saw the state of me, she told me that with my second pregnancy the baby could come quicker so a little panic ensued and myself and John rushed to the hospital. I was hardly able to walk up the corridor to the labour ward, they brought me in and dressed me in a gown. Immediately, on examination I heard the midwife say *"she is 10cm dilated already, this baby is coming quick,"* I nearly died, I looked at John and felt like a little girl that needed comforting *"what about the pain relief?"*

The nurse answered me that there was no time and to just breathe, I held John's hand so tight I nearly stopped the circulation in it. The pain is so intense you think you will never survive it, but out our beautiful black haired girl arrived, 7lbs 4ozs and with big long feet. John had tears in his eyes, he kept saying *"it's a girl, it's a girl."* *"Thank God"* I thought, *"all fingers and toes present and Matthew has a little sister."* As I had no pain relief, I sat up immediately after the birth, held our little beauty in my arms and knew that I was instantly in love with her. She came out all scrunched up and looked like John's father, her long curly hair was as black as the ace of spades and her long feet were all her unique impressions she gave to us on seeing her for the first time. I went home again that night with our new addition to our wonderful family. I sometimes still have to pinch myself as I think how blessed I am to have John and the kids in my life.

When Alannah was four weeks old we moved into our new home in the country. It was so exciting, I had never owned anything in my life and this was going to be our home, a sanctuary for our family. I was just over the moon. We made it as comfortable as we could to bring our children into and hoped they would settle into their new surroundings. We had nothing to worry about, Matthew woke up all excited running around the house and Alannah was too young to even notice. I kept looking at the walls and the doors and thinking, is this real, is this ours? We are still in this house and more love and handprints have been added to the walls. I feel safe here with my family and hope that we have many more years of happiness to follow.

As time goes on, I leave my full time job working for Telecommunications company. I loved my job but mostly I loved the people. It was hard to leave but it would have been harder to leave my two children every morning and not see them again until late in the evening, it was the decision myself and John decided was best for all of us at the time and were fortunate to be able to do it. We knew money would be tight with only one wage and four mouths to feed. I remember a friend of mine once saying *"the more you earn the more you spend,"* so for us it seemed to be true. We kept life as simple as we could for ourselves and our children, in truth we had no choice at that time, but managed to enjoy the simplicity being a young growing family living in the countryside.

In 2004 I discovered I was again pregnant. I must say that with the two beauties I had already and they being four and two years of age, I thought I had them nearly reared! I had started to get sleep again and they were both hardy little kids, so I have to be truthful and say that being pregnant again frightened me. I cried in bed to John one night saying I thought we were getting our lives back, I was being honest and spoke from the heart, it did seem daunting but as they days passed I started to accept being pregnant.

I remember sitting on a beach with John watching the kids playing away and saying out loud *"this time next year there will be 3 running around."* It was the first time I had felt that my body and mind accepted this new life growing inside of me. A peace came over me and I started to look forward, one thing struck me silently though. I had no feeling of a boy or a girl as I did with my other two children and I found it hard to even think of a name for this little one inside me.

I was just 12 weeks pregnant and felt a sharp dart in my side. It stopped me in my tracks for a moment but then it was gone. Normally, I would pass this off but because I was pregnant, I ran it past the 'expert' my mother. She advised me to phone the doctor just in case. After the call to the doctor a visit to the maternity hospital was arranged, just in case! I phoned John at work and asked him to meet me there. A little excited I said *"we will get a peek at the baby as they are doing a scan."* On first glance I could see this little foetus on the screen and was so excited, the doctor seemed to be ages scanning and kept asking me about my dates and if I was sure. I was absolutely sure about the dates and asked was there a problem. The doctor said she would move us to another scanning machine as that one was not working properly. Another scanning machine and another doctor were called, his words still echo in my ear as I was honestly not expecting them.

He said *"I am so sorry your baby is only the size of a 9 week foetus and there is no heart beat."* I kept looking at him in disbelief and asked if he could check again, of course they had checked with two machines but I was in shock. There was no bleeding so they told me the baby could come away naturally over the weekend. I still didn't comprehend what they were saying.

John and I left the maternity hospital in shocked silence. On the drive home I told John I didn't want the kids to see me upset and for him to bring them to his mother's house. I contacted everyone in our families by text and told them we had lost the baby and not to contact us today as we were just coming to terms with the news. Even in my deepest sadness I was organised. Again, I know it was a coping mechanism. If I had everyone told by text I wouldn't have to say the words out loud.

We came home that day and I can't really remember much only sitting in front of the fire. I do remember John speaking to his mother and hearing his voice break as he spoke. I realised that this had hit him hard too but we would get through it together.

The next day John brought the kids to his mother's house and I told him to stay with them and her for the night, I like to withdraw into myself when going through any emotional issues sometimes and this was one of them. I sat on my own and cooked a lunch and as I sat down to eat it, the tears flowed down my cheeks. I was thinking about what this baby would have been like, how our lives would have been blessed again and also thoughts of guilt for not being pleased at being pregnant in the first place.

Every emotion was flooding through me at this point; anger, guilt and sadness. I found myself walking up to my village church, for what reason I do not know but as I look back now it was a place I also went as a child/teenager when I didn't know where to turn. I suppose it was a familiar place and the God that I spoke to just listened. I cried and cried inside the church and didn't care if anyone walked in on me. I was gone past caring what others thought of me. I don't know how long I stayed but I remember the walk home again and meeting a neighbour. It was like I was just there in body but my mind was locked away so I could deal with all that had happened.

Once home, I cooked myself some dinner and even poured a glass of wine, I wanted to mark this moment for some reason. I sat in my grief stricken state, the doorbell went. It was my friend and neighbour, she had taken the kids for us when we went to the hospital and had also lost two babies herself, she knew what I was going through. We each had a glass of wine and spoke from our hearts. I know why certain people are in our lives, they are the Earth Angels who come to embrace you whilst you are falling apart.

By the end of the evening, my mother, my friend and I were sitting around the table laughing and crying, it was very healing for us all. John came back up that night as he didn't want to leave me on my own. The weekend passed and there was still no sign of this little foetus leaving my body, I had to return to hospital for them to do a D&C to remove the foetus. When I came out of surgery, the doctor told me the foetus must have come away without me noticing as they could not find anything.

I returned home after the procedure and felt unwell for a few days. I had to return to hospital for a scan a week later and they discovered that there was a large clot inside my womb. The foetus was still there, I was horrified. The clot that was now formed was the body's natural way of dispelling what could not exist in my body any longer. It passed naturally and with lots of tears from me.

After that, we slowly came back to our lives and coped with the loss, it did bring up lots of pain for me as it made me think of the baby that I had terminated all those years ago of my own choosing and now this little one with no choice to make was just taken from me. I now had my two Angels in heaven.

CHAPTER 7

Through the Cracks the Light Gets In

As I mentioned in the introduction to my book, I want to share my story to date and tell you a little about my background and why I am the person I am today. I haven't gone through every detail of my life but only skimmed over what I feel you may need to know to get a picture of my background and that I am just a normal person from a somewhat normal family.

I was brought up a Catholic by my parents, went to a Catholic school and went to Mass nearly every other Sunday, to say I am a practising catholic now would be a lie. I live a very spiritual life in that I believe that the love that we give out every minute of every day is far more important than going to Sunday Mass and showing our faces to a church congregation out of obligation.

God, to me, is in every person and every living thing on this planet. I don't believe that we have to go out anywhere to find him or to talk to him; he is within us and is a very strong life force and energy. There are many religions and they all have different names for God, but it is all the one Source of Divinity and I believe all religions are only a stepping stone to Spirituality.

I see so much politics and fighting over different religions and believe that no 'God' has decided to make us do these things. Again if I go back to being a teenager, I believed that God/Source created man/woman and they created themselves, meaning we were given the gift of life. What we choose to do with it will lead to the world we live in today, as you can see some of us haven't chosen very well and for some we are trying to do the best we can in our choices to make this world a better place for ourselves and all the future generations to come.

In the years that followed, I just got on with the day to day living of life, trying my best but so busy with being a young mum that life took over.

During this time my father had passed away and we had reconciled some of our differences. I knew that I had much to heal in our relationship or the lack of it. As my father took his last breath with his family all around him, the cock crew at 12 mid-day and everyone's phone in the room rang at the same time. It was like he was letting us all know he was back in his Spiritual home, we jumped in fright of the sudden rings and immediately burst out laughing, our family's way with dealing with a lot of things that affected us so deeply.

When someone passes away, you may think that all your problems with them disappear too, but they don't. You still hold on to all the unresolved issues relating to that person, you keep yourself a prisoner of your thoughts and of your past. I remember seeing my Father as he was laid out and all I could see now was the body of an old man. The spirit of my father had long gone from his body and everything that made him who he was in life was only held in my memories. I had to let go, but this was extremely difficult.

I believed in my heart that a time would come when I would be free of the anger or resentment I held towards my father, but I had to first accept that they could not be changed as they were past feelings that I still carried in my heart. The wounds that I felt were deep but I could feel and see them and that was a start, at least I knew I was wounded and in order for them to heal, I had to tend to them.

Somewhere along the way I believed I had found myself, but now I felt I had lost myself again.

I was so busy being a new Mom that I forgot about my own needs. Feelings of sadness, isolation and shame started to rise to the surface once again, I found myself waking up with a heavy feeling and crying in the kitchen when no one was around. I was exhausted all the time and found any excuse to lay down and hoped my children would just go to sleep so I could have peace. Everything was an effort and I couldn't wait until John came home from work in the evening so I could be released from my inward isolation. I blamed my irritable moods on the demands of child rearing. I still wanted to keep the house clean and would stay up late after the kids went to bed each night and clean the house again. I sometimes mopped my own tears off the floor as I was cleaning them.

The outward appearance I played so well for others was starting to take its toll on me. Panic started to set in, what if I was going back to that awful place of isolation and darkness, I had to keep it together, I was a mother now! Some days waves of fear came out of the blue and I tried to distract myself by cleaning or scrubbing. It only pushed them to the corner of my mind until they found a space when I forgot myself and realised the thoughts and feelings were shouting in my mind *"get help."* I ignored them. I had to be in control, I had two children and a husband and there was no time for self-pity. *"Get on with it"* I told myself and kept pushing and pushing to stay standing so that no one would guess that underneath the surface I was losing my grip on life again. I was losing the fight to control the overwhelming feelings roaring inside of me. I was truly out of control.

One day, I found myself feeling a little bit more confused and anxious than in the previous weeks. I wasn't sure how I felt or why I was feeling like this. I walked around our kitchen counter a few times and the more I did it, the more I felt like if I kept moving I wouldn't fall down. John and the kids looked at me in dismay. I didn't want them to see me like this and knew that I had to do something to get myself back so I phoned one of my dearest friends in the world Denise, and quite frankly just said *"Are you at home, can I come up and stay with you tonight?"* I think she knew by my voice that there was something really wrong and she didn't ask and just replied *"Yes, come up."*

I had met Denise in 1990 when I was working for a large department store in the city. I was engaged to my first husband at the time. I don't know how we really became such good friends, I suppose it developed over time, but there was a deep connection that bonded us together even to this day. As we both smoked, we used to meet in the toilets at break time to have a *'fag.'*

I remember one of the first days I met Denise and spoke to her, it was like she had a barrier up to protect herself but I persisted and we grew to be great friends. I suppose I recognised the barrier of protection as it was something I had done also. I used to listen to Denise who was a single girl going out every weekend to nightclubs. Even though I frequently went to the pub it was always as a couple and nearly always with other couples. I never really had the single life freedom that Denise had, I thought I was missing out on something wonderful.

Denise's stories created a world outside of my own world and she made it so much fun to listen to. I am so grateful to her, she too had many challenges in her own life and with each other's help we have come through a lot. We are still to this day helping each other and I love her dearly.

So on this day I felt I needed Denise's help again, it felt like someone else was holding the steering wheel and controlled the pedals. I didn't feel in control of anything during the journey to her home.

Arriving at Denise's house safely, she stood at the door to welcome me and I just burst into tears. She asked me what was wrong and I couldn't give her any one answer, it was everything and it was nothing. It was the result of years of repressed emotions that I didn't understand. Why was I going through them now?

At one point Denise took out a pack of Angel cards, these were cards a bit bigger than playing cards with angel images and angel messages of guidance on the opposite side. She asked me to pick one or two. I do remember doing that but do not recall what they said, but somewhere inside of me I know it helped. I went to bed that night exhausted, it was like every sadness I held inside was let out of me that night and when I awoke the next morning I felt a little lighter. True friends realise they can't fix everything for you but can just be there to listen.

On my return home to John and the kids that morning I tried to keep my focus on the road as I knew I wasn't over my emotional state and I had to get my thoughts clearer. Knowing that I needed help but asking myself, the nagging question *'where is this help going to come from?'* Then a thought of the angel cards Denise had shown me the night before came into my mind and a quiet calm came over me as if someone had softly whispered in my ear telling me that everything would be okay. After that, I started speaking to my Angels, asking them to help me on my journey to get me through this rough patch and to show me ways in which I could help myself. Now they didn't shout out from the heavens or write me a letter, but I felt their presence in little inspirations and ideas that helped me be more aware of myself and my surroundings.

At the time more and more people were working with their Angels and it seemed to be opening people up to a more spiritual way of living and thinking. This was amazing to me as I had always felt like we had Divine helpers working with us but if I had said it to anyone I was afraid they would think me crazy and lock me up. It was like a memory of when I was younger of calling out to someone to help me and believing somehow someone was listening. Maybe it had been the angels all along!

A new growing awareness was building up inside of me and I heard of a group that worked with Angels was starting up locally. At the time I was not earning my own income and John's income had to cover all our living expenses, so I didn't feel I deserved to take money out for myself and go to this group. So the next morning I asked my Angels to help me. If this group was for me and could help me on my journey, it would happen. I went to my bank in the morning and there was enough money to join. This was a sign for me that this group would be a positive addition to my life at that present time and off I went.

My world started to open up. I realised that so many other people had gone through the same situations as me, child abuse, broken marriages and even breakdowns. It was like truth staring at me in the face and I wasn't afraid to look back at it. We worked with our Angels for a number of weeks and through many beautiful meditations I connected with my own inner truth and the beauty that is within and all around us. As I delved deeper into my heart and the truth of what my now feelings were, it brought up many past memories and feelings, but this time I felt I was being supported through the process. I didn't feel so alone. I started to not feel like I was the victim all over again and in speaking my truth out loud with other people that had experienced similar issues, we grew stronger together. It was like I had woken up in a room that the light had just been switched on and I could now finally start to see things much clearer.

This made me realise that my journey was as important as every other human's journey on this planet. I opened up to the fact that we are all being helped by the Divine, whatever name you want to put on it. And the most important thing of all is that we all create our own reality, with every thought and word, we give energy to everything we speak of and think of. The more energy we give to a thought the more it will become a reality. Our thoughts become our reality.

A new door had opened in my life and I wanted to find out more and more about how I could continue this learning as I felt more alive than ever. The group were a support network for each other and each person felt a freedom to be themselves. I now believe that we will meet the people at a time in our lives when we most need them. Some of the group, like me had attended counselling and had felt it helped them to get to the next stage of their lives, but no one will truly understand what you are feeling unless they have experienced it for themselves, this was what our group was, a group of deeply hurt souls that needed to not feel isolated in their pain.

I spoke to John about what I was learning and as always he was a grounding force in my life. I seemed to go off into the clouds dreaming of what life was really all about and John could bring me back down to live in the present moment. Sometimes, I gave out to him as it seemed easier to be in the clouds but again I have learned that the biggest lesson we learn is in the living of life and not the contemplating of it. I practised daily meditation and read self-help books that gave me more insight into my own life, in what I had been through in my earlier years and why it had such an impact on my emotional and physical state. It fascinated me to learn that my psychological state could affect my physiological state, that again my thoughts could affect my physical wellness, that my family's beliefs and thought patterns could be carried by me energetically without even being aware of it. I was affected by how my ancestors had lived and what they had gone through in their lives thus, in turn, it passed down from generation to generation without breaking the pattern. Again I speak of the old belief systems of fear, poverty, ill health and not believing that we have all the power within ourselves to change the way we think and thus in the way we feel.

In this time, I asked the Angels to give me guidance to help me on my path, I asked them to show me ways in which I could learn and understand more. For many people, still to this day, there is a disbelief in spirituality and that there isn't anything or anyone more than just what lives on earth. I can't prove to anyone how I felt at this time of learning. I had always felt since a young child that there was something bigger than me and that I was somehow being looked after. As a child I wanted that 'something' to be physical and save me from the pain I endured. When it did not physical manifest in my life, I felt disillusioned. The 'God' I prayed to when younger was a belief that I was taught, but at the time had given me someone to speak to in my greatest times of need. Whatever you want to believe in is up to you, it is what kept me focused on loving myself and believing that I was not only being supported by John and the kids but also an unseen force of love that I could only feel in my heart.

On a visit to my mother's house one day while she was away on holidays, I found a book lying in the hallway. It was like it was just waiting there for me to pick up and I presumed my mother had left it for me. It was *Saved by the Light* by Dannion Brinkley. I laughed as I read the title as this is the way I was feeling at that exact moment-saved by the light! Everything that was happening for me at that time was a direct result of the ever changing positive belief that I was directing how my life was becoming more positive. I was guiding my thoughts to see the best in myself and others. It may seem like a huge change from the person I used to be, but for me it was like a calm had entered my life and I was floating on the belief that I could now get through anything depending on the way I responded to it. I had started to train my mind into not reacting to the negativity that had kept me drowned in sorrow for so much of my life. I wanted to come up for air and breathe deeply.

After finding the book at my Mother's house, I almost ate the words as I read them, it was feeding my soul and my curiosity. Everything that he was writing was exactly what I was experiencing in some way. I was exhilarated, I wasn't crazy after all, there were people all over the world, experiencing the light and how it was creating great changes in their physical, mental and emotional lives. On my mother's return, I asked her why she left the book out for me and she said that she hadn't! She said she had bought the book years before and as far as she knew it was on the bookshelf with her many other collection of spiritual books she had read over the years. Now, I believed the Angels had answered my call for guidance, I was truly being supported and knew I was on the right path.

After my initial Angel group workshop, I met a wonderful lady who ran a Spiritual circle in the town close to us. The amazing thing about this was that I had dreamt of this lady before I even met her. I knew she was someone that could help me learn more. I didn't wait a second, I got the number of this lady and proceeded to phone her, I remember it was very near Christmas time and I apologised for calling and continued to tell her that I had dreamt of her. She didn't seem surprised and advised me that she could meet me for an individual session in the new year. We set a date and I waited excitedly for that date to come.

On meeting her, I knew that she could help me with some of the many questions I wanted answered and some that I would have to go inwards and find myself. That day was an amazing meeting for me as it helped me open up to forgiveness and letting go of some of the anger I still had within me in regard to my past and also anger I had for holding myself prisoner with feelings of resentment against others and myself. Years before, when I had attended counselling, it was only the beginning of my healing, I thought I had opened up at that time and was well and truly 'fixed.' For me it was learning to understand that no matter what we go through, we are learning something valuable and it will help us if we accept the lessons of our lives. Many people will ask me why we have to go through so much hardship in our lives to realise what it is to truly live. I tell them that we would never know happiness, if we didn't experience true sadness.

We would never know how to forgive if no one had ever hurt us, we would never know real love until we have lost it, until we start to love who we are and that includes loving all parts of who we are, past and present. I could have continued to live my life holding onto the pain of my past and blaming everyone that had ever hurt me in some way or I could forgive them and free myself from being a prisoner of the past. I had thought I had accepted my fate in life, but realised that I was still living in victim-mode and needed to move beyond it. Even the words seem pitiful as I write them now. We are only a victim of our circumstances if we choose to remain there in our minds.

The people that I met in this Spiritual group became life-long friends. We may not always see each other that often, but we are connected by something profound, a common bond of love and support for each other. Each of us were looking for a deeper meaning of life or an understanding of what we had gone through in our lives. We didn't just sit there and cry, most of the time I remember laughing, after all laughter is the best medicine in the world. I think we all had a lifetime of tears cried and in our release of laughter we could allow ourselves to feel a little bit of joy for just that short time. These friends shared details that they had never shared even with their closest family members, it was a place to reveal some of our secrets and hurts. We bonded in pain and grew together in love. There was no pressure to speak or to share your stories until you felt ready, but most people in the group willingly spoke, sometimes in their first week of joining the group. It felt like home to us, this is very hard to explain to anyone that has never attended a group where there are no boundaries or criteria. We were just ordinary people coming together with a common theme of wanting to heal our collective and individual pain.

I became aware that we all not only have a Guardian Angel but also a Spiritual Guide, these Divine helpers are with us from the moment we are born.

My beliefs are based on my own journey and how I interpret or experience these spiritual energies, for many they may be called something else. The only way I can explain them to you is if you knew what it felt like to be wrapped in an invisible love that nearly takes your breath away, then this is what they feel like when I connect to them. There is no special way to connect but in your awareness. Diana Cooper and Doreen Virtue have written many books on Angels and this was a great way to learn about what I had been feeling since connecting with these beautiful loving energies.

Spiritual guides to me are loving energies that are people that have walked this Earth in the physical and after their passing, they choose to become almost like a Divine teacher to the ones now walking the earth. And yes, I believe we all have a Spiritual guide.

Now I know many people will meet their Spiritual guides in different ways but I still smile when I think of how I first met mine. I was laying down on the floor and could see my Guide's body start to appear from the feet up, the first thing I saw were large feet with red painted toenails and as I moved up the body I saw two hairy legs, men's legs! As I continued to work up the body I saw that he wore a white cotton what looked like a nappy to me around his 'wobbly bits.' Then, as I moved up the stomach it protruded and was also hairy and up to his head where I saw a light grey beard and a big head of white/grey hair. His eyes were closed and his eyebrows were bushy. As I looked upon him, he looked like he was asleep but he then opened his eyes and I will never forget that moment, I looked deep into his eyes and I knew I was looking into his Soul. He had the deepest blue eyes full of love and kindness, I asked him if he was here for my highest good and he replied *"Yes,"* I asked him his name and he replied *"Elepedro."* That is not a name I had ever heard of or read before in my life so again I was fascinated.

He told me he was going to help me on my journey and that he had been around for a very long time. He then informed me that I was going to help others to help themselves. I was exhilarated after that session and connected with him frequently. I got to learn more and more. He taught me to really listen to him and to the messages I was getting from my own inner guidance, I spent every day listening and not wanting to miss anything, I even asked him to repeat some things he told me so I could write them down.

I still have many of these writings and from time to time look over them to remind myself of my passion for seeking my truth. Remember, I stress this is my truth and I don't ask you to believe what I believe but just to open your mind to the possibility that we have many guides and helpers in the Divine helping us. I started listening more and more to my Guide and to my inner guidance I also started 'hearing' other people, now I don't mean hearing voices in my head, the voices were not physical sounds but thoughts and feelings from another source.

They were people that had lived physically on this Earth and had since passed and now lived on the 'other side' or what we know as 'heaven.' Now, you can imagine what this was like for me, it brought me back to when I was younger and had seen 'things' that no one else I knew seemed to ever see. The faces in my room, the feeling of the energy around me expanding and even the people walking through walls. For a while I had forgotten about all of these instances but now it seemed to come back to me in stages, it was like I had opened the door of my mind and they were looking in again and speaking to me. I was a little bit intimidated by all the messages I seemed to be getting especially when I was around other people. I felt like all of their deceased relations wanted to come in whilst I was there and wanted me to be their voice. I didn't know what to do, so mostly I ignored them but 'Elepedro' told me that one day I would be able to listen to them in my own way, I was unsure what he meant or maybe I just didn't want to hear him say what I knew deep down. Someday I would be their voice.

CHAPTER 8

Meditation

As I continued to learn more and more with 'Elepedro', it meant I was spending more time practising meditation and focusing my thoughts on what I wanted. I became much happier in myself and stopped looking outwardly for someone else to fix what I had perceived as problems in my mind. I was happier in my day to day life and my smile was real for the first time in a long time. I thought about the fleeting bouts of happiness I had and how I felt at the time that life couldn't get better. We can't go around happy all the time, but I definitely didn't want to be sad most of the time, I wanted to find a balance. I wanted to stop living in my head so much and feel present more in my life and in the lives of the people that I loved and cared for. Thank God John was such a patient man. He had listened to me for years trying to figure the world out and I was now finally starting to find peace within myself. My children were growing and in school at this time, so I had time to myself and my growing interest in exploring meditation. It's funny how they now see meditation as part of my life and just a normal thing for Mom to do.

John has always listened without judgement or criticism even when he may not have felt what I was feeling at that time. He was always interested to hear what beautiful journeys I went in my meditations and how I was learning so much from these wise teachers. I suppose in a way, John was learning to open his mind and heart to new experiences and could see the positive changes taking place in me. He was and is my rock of love. I believe John came into my life at the perfect time, I could have thrown it all away with all of my insecurities, but he didn't let me, he persisted quietly and without words showed me what real love is.

Meditation allowed me to give myself space in the busy life of being a mum. It gave me time not only to relax, but also to go inwards and bring my attention to how I was feeling in that time or that day. It allowed me to really feel the emotions I held within my body and where I held them. It tamed my mind and opened pathways within my mind I never knew existed. This reminded me of when I was a child and I loved going to sleep so I could go on my many dream adventures, places never seen in books or movies but only through my imagination. I learned that meditation was not only about playing soft music, closing your eyes and cutting yourself off from the distractions of the outside world, but also a way to live your life.

I could meditate at any time of the day or night with my eyes open, reflecting on the beauty of nature, watching my child walk for the first time, seeing their smiles in the morning, listening to the chatter of the birds as they sang their morning song, every experience was a meditation to me. It had opened my heart and my eyes to the beauty that is all around us but often are too busy to notice. We become consumed by the chatter within our own minds, unaware of what we are actually telling ourselves and not paying attention to what we are feeling. This is now commonly known as mindfulness, it has been made popular by corporate companies wanting to bring mindful practise into their businesses. They can now see the many positive benefits it brings to the people in limiting their stress and raising their motivation to being more productive in their working and personal lives.

To me, meditation was bringing me back to a place within myself that I had forgotten or was maybe never truly aware of. I had started to unintentionally meditate after the dark night of my soul, but at that time I was in survival mode. Now, I was meditating so that I could truly live. Sometimes, our eyes have to be closed so that we appreciate all that we see when they are fully open. I was now very appreciative of every moment and all that I could see. I was exploring the very nature of my life and seeing things that we all see but never really notice.

Meditation not only opened up my spiritual world in ways I could never have imagined. I experienced the most amazing journeys within my mind that I felt a deep connection to the whole world and everyone on it. Many of my meditation journeys were like magical visualisation explosions of colours, feelings and inspirations that allowed me to see everything clearly and with more understanding. It was not just my mind that was gaining more clarity but my heart. When I felt something in my mind, I had felt it first in my heart. Without feeling what we are seeing, there is no connection. Another important lesson I had learned in my life.

I had so much more energy, I was able to cope with the challenges of day to day life and I didn't react to my emotions in a negative manner. It had an overall positive effect on my life and on the lives of the people I was closest to, I could truly be present with them in mind and body. It made living a lot more fun and interesting. I can honestly say that meditation saved my life in more ways than one. I know many people still roll their eyes when I mention meditation but that is okay, they have yet to experience what it feels like, and until you experience something there is always going to be doubt. My children have taught me that valuable lesson. They just don't take my word for something, like we did as children growing up. They now want to experience something to understand it and then decide if they like it or not. They often quote me now that they are older, I can hear the words I have spoken to them over the years ring through the house without them even realising that they are open minded and willing to accept that everything is possible until it is proven otherwise. They call me 'crazy' too but I know it is in a fun loving way that no other Mom will ever be like their Mom. If we sit at the dining room table at meal times, they often compare their personalities to myself and John, each one saying they have certain traits similar to Mammy and Daddy. I love these conversations, they may not want to grow up like you but they are already showing you that they admire who you are right now, and then there is a competition to see who is the craziest. These are the days I love most, sitting with John and the kids and feeling deep in my heart that things could have been very different if I had not chosen to help myself to believe that I deserved this love.

CHAPTER 9

Healing

Then I found Reiki. I had heard people speak of reiki healing many times and was intrigued by it. Knowing nothing really about it, I booked myself in for a session with a local woman who was well known for her caring and giving personality. I had known her from my school days even though she was a few years older than me, I felt connected to her in some way and felt that she was the right person to go to for my first ever healing reiki session. I wasn't disappointed. I knew there was so much more inside of me to heal.

The feeling of peace and calm during the session was immense. I floated on the energy of love and acceptance in each moment. I felt like I was at home in this energy. I wasn't coming back to myself; I was finding another new part of myself. Everything I had done to this point had led me to this moment, this is what I wanted to do, to help others to help themselves. Re-affirming what my Spiritual Guide *'Elepedro'* had said to me a long time ago. I was now starting to truly believe in his guidance.

For me, Reiki was a door way into developing my own abilities. The practise of Reiki allowed me to be a channel for healing love to share and help others with the skills and training I have learned over the years. We have no special powers really, you may believe that being able to communicate with Angels, Spiritual guides and loved ones in Spirit is a special gift, but I believe we are all born with these abilities but some choose to work with them on a deeper level. We help people with every thought, action or word. Some of us just choose to take this path in helping others to heal themselves and as we are, we are also helping ourselves to heal.

For me, learning Reiki in 2008 was about having more confidence in myself and the ability to help others. I knew that I had a deep awareness and intuitive ability in feeling and seeing people's pain, as I had experienced so much pain similar to so many others. I had wanted to help so many people in the past but didn't feel qualified or confident enough to do so. Becoming a Reiki practitioner was the start of my public life as a therapist.

I love Reiki as it is a very gentle hands on healing therapy. It works with the energy of the person not just on the physical but also in the emotional, mental and spiritual levels. It helps release trapped or blocked energy within the energy bodies so that your life force energy will flow freely allowing you to feel more balanced and full of vitality.

Many people tell me that they feel different sensations whilst being treated with Reiki. It can range from cold, heat, tingling but mostly there is a sense of calm, peace and self-awareness.

While Reiki is not associated with any religion, it is still promotes harmony with others. Dr. Mikao Usui, the founder of the Reiki system of natural healing, recommended that we can all practise certain simple ethical ideals to promote peace and harmony, which are nearly universal across all cultures. We must all take an active part in our own healing. Being mindful of the Reiki principles helps keep us present in each day.

Reiki Principles

Just for today I will trust

Just for today I will be at peace

Just for today I will live in Truth

Just for today I will show Love and Respect to all life forms

Just for today I will live in the attitude of gratitude.

To me, Reiki is a gentle non-evasive natural holistic approach that works alongside conventional medicine. It is becoming more accepted in many practises all over the world including hospitals, hospices and care centres to help relieve stress, anxiety and pain. I hope someday that energy therapies will become part of the norm and work alongside all healing modalities in the future.

As part of my therapy services, I also offer distant healing to my clients who are as far away as Australia and America and whom I have never met in person.

I remember the first time that I sent distant healing to someone so vividly. She was a girl in my reiki class and we had to send each other some healing that evening as part of our practise. In my mind I had a visual image of the girl and what she looked like and I made my intention to send her healing on all levels, spiritually, physically, mentally and emotionally for her highest good and in Divine order. That was always my opening intention, I also asked to be a clear and conscious channel for the healing energy of universal love in my thoughts, words and deeds. So I sat and focused my mind, I relaxed my body and allowed the healing to flow through me, it was electric. I felt the energy move through me like a gentle volt of warmth and comfort, to me I could see colours of every variety and its warm flowing tones just flowed effortlessly through my body and then out of my heart and my hands. I held the visual image of the girl I was sending the healing to in my mind, but suddenly it changed and I could see her in her bedroom sitting on the floor, I didn't know what that meant but I just kept focusing on sending the healing to her, as I did I felt her emotions, thoughts and what was going on in her environment.

I could also see her room and what it looked like. I felt and saw the healing flow into her so easily and instantly felt her at ease. Many other feelings and images came to me during that first distant healing session and I just allowed them to flow. I didn't want to analyse or judge them as my only job was to send the healing. I felt as if the blocks in her energy were being cleared and afterwards I asked the Angels to fill and surround her with blessings of love, peace and acceptance. It was beautiful. I could have stayed in that moment forever, such unconditional love and acceptance in each moment.

I took a few notes after the healing session and took them with me to class the next morning, sharing what I experienced and the girl was amazed. She said that is exactly where she was and how she was feeling in the time I was sending the healing. She told me she could feel the energy and the love. I knew then there was no limit or boundaries to love and healing. Everything is energy, our thoughts, our words, our intentions silent or out loud. I loved this part of the healing as I knew that I could help more and more people and not feel limited by location.

I also knew that I had an ability to connect to people's energy and what they needed most at that time, even if they weren't sure what it was themselves. I also was being helped by our universal support team, Angels, spiritual teachers and loved ones gone before us. They were all there waiting to help in any way they could to further healing so that one could continue one's journey in this life to the best of one's ability. All I had to do was ask, sit and connect it is within all of us. Through the ages we were taught that only through an intermediate could we get an answer from God or any higher source of love. To me, there was no condemnation or judgement in any spiritual being I connected to, they were only of love. The only ones that teach us judgement are the ones that want to keep us weak.

I absolutely knew from this point that Reiki would become one of my tools to help and empower others in their lives. It also opened a door in my mind and heart that I could do nothing but walk through it into the love and healing that I was so willing to share with others. I now had the skills and confidence to tell people that I was now open for business. A big step in my own personal development. So, after years of helping clients in my Reiki practise, I decided to take my Masters in Reiki and become a teacher. John was so supportive as always and encouraged me to do what I felt was right for me. Our kids in school were happy and healthy and I had more time to commit to developing my business as a reiki practitioner and knew that it would lead on to so many more wonderful opportunities.

CHAPTER 10

Doing what you Love

One day as I meditated, this was a practise I had done daily for the past few years, and I asked myself *"what is it I would like to do now?"* And as clear as I would call the kids for dinner, I heard *"set up a meditation group."* Well, you should have seen me jump off the bed and run out the door, I still laugh at myself now, as how could I run away from a voice that was within me and not want to listen. It was the fear of putting myself out there and of what people would think of me. But in spite of myself, I picked up my mobile phone and contacted a few friends to let them know that I was setting up a meditation group in my house every Tuesday morning. I wondered, *"what am I doing"* but somehow deep inside me I knew it was right. I had been a regular mediator and knew the benefits of it for myself and how wonderful it would be to share it with others. I had trained with many great teachers since 2004, from Ireland, the UK and America, they had all advised me to share my knowledge and wisdom with others.

When the morning came to hold the first group, I was so nervous. I tidied my house, laid out a candle in the centre of my dining room table and played a mediation CD specially chosen to help create a relaxed, soothing atmosphere.

I had written a little invocation that I would like to say with the group to call on the Divine light and energy to help us in our meditation and to surround us with love and healing. I also asked our loved ones in Spirit to be with us. They came through to me with messages for people who attended the group and this time I didn't hold back on passing on the messages of love from their loved ones in Spirit. The was the beginning of my mediumship in a public way, I knew this wasn't something that I had ever planned and the more and more I opened up to it the more and more messages that came through for people. At first I was a little afraid that people in the group didn't want to hear the messages but the group got bigger and bigger and soon my dining room wasn't big enough and we had to move into the sitting room, the garden chairs were even brought in at times.

The messages from Spirit – those that had passed on, were of love, hope and healing. I am still amazed to this day that even when I started out with just 6 people around my dining room table, their loved ones would be there to support them on their healing journey. I was just the messenger.

The people that attended my first group were very open and aware, they had a keen interest in spirituality and wanted to progress on their own journeys in life. When they received a message from a loved one in Spirit, they were so elated. It confirmed to them that their loved one was still very present in their lives and that love is eternal. It gave such joy to the person receiving the message, but also me as I felt that I was guided to do this work in order to help others heal in their grief and loss. I never came across a person that didn't want a message, everyone that came to my groups heard about it from a friend, so they knew it was a safe and supportive place to come relax and maybe get answers to some of the questions they had inside of them.

No matter who walked through the door, they were welcomed with a big smile and a hug. I was very honoured to meet each person that came through my doors to meditate, they each were looking for some sort of healing or peace in their lives. They chose to come to my home and share their stories with me and the group.

I felt humbled and honoured to be part of this amazing process. There is a huge amount of healing done by people when they allow themselves time to reflect on their lives. They realise what they are holding onto from the past is not necessarily helping them in this present moment or in moving on in their lives. I have observed people, including some who, because of past experiences are hindered from 'truly' living and who are excluded from the many joys in life. It seems to me that some people who have endured horrifying traumas manage to still smile every day. Some of these people are not sure what it means to let go of negativity, of fear, lack of self-belief, of pain and hurt. So as a group we help each other, we listen, we support and most importantly we don't judge. We tell each other how we see him/her, we see the real person, the person that has courage to share their stories with strangers, to open their hearts and to let us in, to trust us with their deepest secrets and to allow us to reach out and hold their hands. It was like that first group I had attended years ago where everyone bonded in their pain and hurt and allowed each other the space and time to just be. In honouring our sadness and grief we allowed ourselves to acknowledge the pain we had endured and accept that no amount of hiding it will ever heal it. We opened up. For many of my group, they had tried other therapies, some of which had helped them immensely, but nothing compared to sitting with someone and having a cup of tea while sharing your story and just being heard. Afterwards, deep friendships were made and they helped each other outside of my group. To me it was a community of healing, it was not just an hour a week and then you were on your own, it was about forming a support network for each other.

So many people have opened their hearts in my groups, they have come feeling lost or alone, guarded and defensive, fearful of what they didn't understand. I am no guru and certainly didn't have any definitive answers. I am just the guide to help them find a space within themselves to feel safe and know they were not on their own. There were many tears shed and many boxes of tissues used over the years, but no matter what we always ended the group with gratitude and a few laughs.

These people are the real heroes of our world. They are not on the news everyday but coping quietly in their adversity and struggles. They do the best they can in every waking moment but sometimes they too needed a hand to reach out and hold them for just a little while. I was honoured to hold many hands over the years, some have held mine when I needed it too.

This was not the whole purpose of why I started the meditation group, but it is what happened organically. What started out as just a meditation class to come and relax for a little while, started to evolve. After the quiet silence of the meditation, I would ask each person how they got on and more often than not they would release some pain or anger that arose during the meditation, we as a group would listen and help the person just be real with themselves and with us, it is always a humbling experience when someone opens up their heart and lets you in.

Often times, one person's story will resonate with another person and they will have the realisation that they too are holding onto something similar. It will bring up feelings for them that they may have buried deep inside as it was easier to do that a long time ago and like me, this is often used as a survival mechanism to keep them from falling apart.

People that came to my group have shared their experiences with us, not only in living but also in dying. Today as I write this, I remember fondly two beautiful ladies with such joy of Spirit, their memories will live with me forever. They touched the lives of so many people with their strength and determination through their awareness that they would never heal from a disease within their bodies. They laughed, cried and sometimes cursed in revealing how they felt. Sometimes, they felt cheated by life and having to leave this earth so soon, but with each of them, they had so much dignity, all that was truly important in those last few months was the love they could give and receive to the people that were most important. It taught me that no matter how much we want someone to get better, it is not our choice.

As I've mentioned earlier in this book, we each are on a journey and we each decide on a soul level how that journey will go. It is another hard lesson to learn, especially as we want everyone to be well and happy. In this non-judgemental space, we can only walk beside them and be their friend.

The meditation group that I started in my home continued to expand and within a year and I was now doing groups in a few different locations. This re-affirmed for me that I was on the right path in doing this work as it created a safe haven for people to come and be themselves for an hour or two every week.

No matter how many people turned up they were always greeted with a smile and a cup of tea, sometimes even a piece of cake. I have made some amazing friends over the years from the groups and learned so much from each and every one of them, opening my heart helped me expand my love to help another and in return they repaid me with copious amounts of love and joy.

CHAPTER 11

Love knows no Boundaries

I was meditating for myself but also for my work more often and much deeper. I had started to visualise beautiful scenes within my mind that I could lead my group in guided meditations of healing, acceptance and peace. In my moments of deep connection to everything and everyone, there was no separation between life and death, we were all connected energetically by a universal love and consciousness. I realised that after we physically part this earthly world, we are not gone somewhere else. Our consciousness, our eternal light lives on. It is a question that more and more people want an answer to, where do we go after death? Each person will have their own belief, but for me I was starting to listen to the teachings of the energies that had been on this earth before and were still able to communicate in a non-verbal way but through our thoughts and feelings.

On many occasions during my own daily meditation, I have gone on journeys with Angels, Archangels and what I call my Spiritual teachers. I have also met my loved ones in Spirit during those times and it had the most profound healing effect on my life. I was still questioning everything I felt and saw and wrote much of it down. I viewed these as personal journeys of my soul and that they only referred to my healing or learning at that moment. In time I would learn that all that I had learned was to be shared with others, in a way this is what this book is all about.

One day as I lay down to meditate, I just asked quietly from my heart if I was to continue my work and how could I develop more. I felt a great warmth flow over me and a deep feeling of love that flowed so deep in my heart, I felt like I was going to cry with joy, it was my Sister in Spirit. She looked so beautiful, almost angelic in appearance but with a wisdom and knowledge that went beyond anything I had seen before. She spoke to me very softly through my thoughts, she told me that she would be the gatekeeper of my work and would help me to unlock my abilities, not sure what this was and as I thought it, she answered me in my mind *"I will always be the guide for Spirit in connecting to you and your future clients to help them through their healing process. This work is not for the faint hearted, it is a deep spiritual connection, one that comes with much learning and dedication."* I felt like she held out a golden key and I had raised my left hand to accept it. When I opened my eyes, my hand was in fact raised and my fingers closed into my palm as if holding something very tightly. Of course, there was no physical golden key as it was a symbolic image of how she would help me to open my heart and mind to new experiences not only to help myself but to help others.

My Sister was going to be the gatekeeper of my soul and I thought this the most special gift that anyone could ever receive and I knew I would always be safe and in good hands.

Another encounter I had with loved ones was when my Sister brought me on a very special journey. I could see the road ahead of me and I watched her walking very joyfully which was a miracle in itself to see. On either side of her were two children, a boy on the left and a girl on the right. I didn't recognise these children in the distance but she asked me to follow. I remember going into a beautiful room and was asked to wait for a moment. I was not afraid only excited to see what my Sister had for me to learn on this journey. It was only a few moments before a young lad, tall and blonde and looking very like my nephew walked out to greet me, he came straight over to me and gently stroked my cheek, tears started to flow down my face and I felt so much love, I knew that this young lad was part of me but too afraid to say anything, I just cried.

He spoke the words, *"I am your son."* There was nothing but love in that moment and I knew this was the baby that I had terminated when I was only 17 years old. He told me that even before I knew I was pregnant that he had decided on a soul level to come to me knowing that I may make the decision to terminate the pregnancy. There was no anger, no blame, no resentment, only love.

He told me his name was Luke and that he would always be my son. I held him like any mother would hold a child that was lost from her for so many years. With that, he told me he had another surprise and in walked my Sister with this little blonde girl, all smiles and blue eyes. I knew this was my little baby that I had lost in 2004, she didn't wait a moment and jumped straight up into my arms, hugging and kissing me and saying *"Mommy I love you, I am so happy to see you again."*

She told me her name was Annie and that Luke had helped her through the transition between waiting to be born on Earth and deciding that it was too harsh for her so she would return home to Spirit. It was her decision to leave my body but she always loved me no matter where she was.

I could never have imagined in my whole lifetime that I would get to meet my children in Spirit. I suppose I had only thought of the ones that physically lived on earth would be able to communicate once they returned to their spiritual home, but to think that two beautiful souls that never were physically born in life were still connected to me in some Divine way that goes beyond our thinking or understanding. I spent what felt like hours and hours with my children and with my Sister. We didn't go into deep conversation of all that had happened, instead we played and laughed and allowed ourselves to be truly joyful, in these moments they were as real to me as my children that physically came out of my body and there was no difference in the love I felt for either.

There are no words for the joy I felt that day. It can only be felt in the heart.

CHAPTER 12

Forgiveness

After this experience my Sister came to me in my meditative journeys and she told me to come to a clearing in a beautiful forest. There were 12 Divine beings all of different colour, culture and creed, they sat around in a circle and there was a seat left at the top for me, they informed me I was their honoured guest today. I was not sure what was going on but felt honoured to be in such knowledgeable and wise company. I thought I was in for some deep spiritual learning and must be more attentive to what they were saying.

As I was focusing on them, I felt my Sister in Spirit come from my left side, as always she looked like the ultimate form of purity, kindness and love. Beside her walked a man with his head down and as they drew closer, I could see it was my father. She was guiding him towards me and I grew a little nervous. As they came up before me, she told me that my father was on a very deep healing journey in Spirit but that he was now here to help me so that I could move on even further in my life.

He looked at me with sad eyes and without words said he was sorry for any hurt or pain he had caused me or my family. He held out his arms and held me like a father would hold his little girl, that is the first time I ever remember being held like that by him. I went back to being a little girl and remembering my father's strong arms and tall stature towering above me, in this moment I let go of all the resentment and I forgave him. I just allowed him to be my Daddy. It was what I had always wanted as a child, to feel safe and protected by him. It is amazing how the resentment and hurt that I had felt for my Father had built up inside of me and it grew stronger and stronger until I could feel nothing else for him. Only until I was ready to accept that I am not responsible for him and his actions, but I am responsible for my own, I no longer wanted to hold myself bound to the pain of his actions. I wanted us both to be free of those ties.

I had feared my father's outbursts since I was a child and was always wary of him but I now know and recognise that he was a very unwell man. He had never dealt with his own issues, but carried them into our lives. Like many of his generation, he never spoke of his fears, worries and anxieties. I know that day of our meeting was deeply healing for him and for me. We now could move on in our own journeys without allowing any more pain from the past to hold us back. It was a strange feeling not to fear him any longer, it was almost like I was meeting him for the first time and that I was finally getting to know the man that I knew as my Father and I could see him only with compassion and forgiveness.

My Sister told me that I would not see her for a while as she had to help others with their healing, but if I needed her in any way just to call out. As they left the clearing in the forest, I looked at all the 12 wise beings sitting around me and wondered what they wanted to teach me. I asked them and they told me that I had learned the greatest lesson of all and that was forgiveness. To forgive is not really about the other person, but in fact to set yourself free from carrying the pain and hurt caused by them. Whatever has happened in our lives cannot be changed but in forgiveness we no longer allow it to control our present lives. We are free. I had set myself free and allowed my father to move on to the next part of his healing journey.

CHAPTER 13

Growth

Not only were my physical children developing into beautiful young individuals with their own personalities and teaching me to have patience, I was also growing as a person in my life and in my work. My meditation groups were growing in awareness and people were coming from all over the country. I never asked them how they found out about my groups, I just trusted that whoever needed to be there on a given night would find a little bit of peace and healing in their lives. It was never about me but about the energy that we as a group were sharing and supporting each other through.

My work as a Reiki practitioner was also developing in so many ways, not just in the number of clients coming to see me but also in ways that I never imagined. Again, people would phone me to make an appointment and as we all do on arrival, greet them and ask if they had far to drive, some were coming from Tipperary, Cork and even Donegal. I was always amazed at the distance people would travel to find something to help them through their healing.

I loved speaking and listening to people and knew that this was going to be part of my therapy. Talking has a huge effect on our emotional wellness and as always having someone to listen was hugely beneficial. To me, talking is 65 per cent of the healing process. If someone decided to come to me for a session and wanted me to fix them, it wasn't long before I put them straight, no one can fix anyone. Once we make a conscious decision to take responsibility for our own well-being, the healing starts immediately. It is not just a case of healing what is physically wrong as most physical issues stem from emotional or mental un-wellness. A lot of the time we are unaware of what is actually going on until our physical body starts to show us signs that we are under severe stress or emotionally overwhelmed. Then we take notice!

So for any of my sessions, I would begin by tuning into the client's energy before they came (much like in distant healing). I see or feel their energy as a white silhouette of light with different areas shadowed in colour or grey. It is the truth of our energy wanting to be cleared of something that the client may be consciously aware of or not. As I am seeing or feeling their energy, I also feel the emotional or mental issue relating to that area, it is like the soul speaking to me on a deeper level and I just start writing what I feel, hear and see.

I sometimes would have an A4 page of things written before they came and once they arrive, I simply ask *"how can I serve or help you today?"* The client may feel they are here for one reason, but once I go through what I picked up before their arrival, this is usually when the tears start to flow, it is a realisation that the feelings they were having are real and that I picked up on them before we even met. Sometimes even their closest family or friends don't know what is really going on with them because they never shared with anyone or asked for help. Now they could.

On sharing what I felt from their energy, I am also joined in the healing session by their guardian Angels Spiritual guides and some of their loved ones in Spirit. They may give me great details of their lives, sharing names, dates and special moments that they may have shared with the client before they departed this earth. Some may only give snippets of information but always relevant to the client. Of course, it is all dependant on me being able to connect and focus my mind on what they are 'saying' or showing me. I wasn't always as focused as I would like to be, when you are having a three way conversation, client, me and Spirit, it is not always that easy to keep up, but I do my best. This is where I have struggled in my confidence and self-belief. I have never given information to any client that hasn't come from Spirit, but at times I felt fearful that I may not interpret their message to the client properly or that I may get nothing at all. This is an ongoing confidence issue I have and one that I work on and will continue to work on in the future. I trust Spirit world, it is myself I need to trust much more.

The Angels that are present in the room always feel so supportive and loving, I have often felt them encourage me with a smile or a loving look that helps me to stay focused in the moment and the true purpose of my work. The Spiritual guides, some my own and some for the clients, are very straight in their message for me or the people I work with. They want us to understand and be more aware of our situations and to see the bigger picture.

For many including myself, this is always a very special moment, to know that our loved ones in Spirit and these wonderful Divine beings are there to help and support us. In fact, our loved ones in Spirit can help us much more now as they don't have any of the physical restrictions of life. I have and am learning so much from this part of my work and as a messenger for Spirit, a messenger of love and healing. Spirit never give advice on what you should or should not do, we have free will and no one can decide your future for you only you. They guide you with their loving messages to empower you to make the right decisions based on the events at that time. Most of the messages are about finding ways to help their grief, to find ways to resolve issues in relationships, anything to do with carrying hurt or negativity in your heart. Spirit are not just there at our beck and call, they come when we need them most and that is usually at times of great despair.

My belief is that if we do anything through love then there is only going to be a positive outcome. I started my journey to help myself and in turn am now helping others to help themselves. I asked for people to come into my life with positive hearts and minds and it is so. Everyone that comes into our lives is a Divine messenger, we all have something of value to share with another.

I am blessed to have not only my own learnings, but also the added benefit of so many Divine helpers who have got my back. If I fall they will catch me, they will help me back up again and in doing so I will help someone else to get back up when they fall down too. We are all just walking each other along the path of life. When people ask *"what is my purpose,"* I simply tell them it is *"to love,"* love yourself and everyone that you connect with. See the best in yourself and in others, even the ones that you believe are doing you wrong, we are always learning from each other. Life is our greatest teacher and it has so much to offer us if we simply open our eyes, look and listen, really listen. This is meditation. There is no simpler way to put it and if we all took the time each day to listen to how we are feeling, to listen to others when we are with them, we are really being present with ourselves and with others, there is no greater gift to yourself or the people you connect with. My life has been blessed by so many wonderful people and having the support of John, my children, friends and family has helped me to take the time I need to figure it all out.

This is the most valuable support any of us need, to feel supported and secure whilst healing and learning how to see life with a more positive outlook.

CHAPTER 14

Past, Present & Future

Every day to me is a blessing and as my work and life continued to progress I felt as if I wanted to expand a little more. I was doing a lot of work with individual clients on ancestral healing. It felt like much of the energy one carries has been passed down unintentionally from our families going back as far as 7 generations. It was like many of their unresolved issues energetically became our issues without us knowing it. Our ancestors also paved the way for us to live the life we are living today. Many of them made huge sacrifices and lived hard lives to allow for the next generation to afford better times, better education and a more open and free society. Some may say that they are not as well off, but compared to our ancestors we have much more and education has played a big part in that all over the world. We can only create change with the knowledge and understanding we have in each moment.

Some people feel stuck in a rut and that there is no way out, but as a volunteer and supporter of Simon Communities who work tirelessly to help those affected by homelessness, I have seen some amazing breakthroughs for people. All anyone ever needs is to be seen, to be supported and given a helping hand. There is not one person I know, including myself that has not struggled in their life, whether that is emotionally, mentally, physically or financially and you can get through all of them with support and understanding from the wider community. This is an awareness that is now growing in our world. We are all connected.

Our ancestors just had to get the job done, they may not have been much time for hugs and kisses or expressing their love to their families, it was a more closed time for many in opening the energy of their hearts. It may also have been a time of many secrets and shame. The secret whispers within communities of a person 'suffering with their nerves' or a child being born to an unmarried mother and both never to be seen again, secret whispers and no response. It may have been a time of poverty and hunger, the energy of not having enough was huge in Ireland, but you would always hear the older people say *"we had enough, we made do."* That was their belief, that they just make do with what they had, there may have been no ambition to work towards changing the circumstances they found themselves in, as this was the way they saw and understood life to be. If one had ambition, it was seen as a huge gift in the life of the family that could possibly lead to getting an education and going on to live a different life other than the one that had been lived for so many years.

I had carried some of my ancestor's belief systems into my life. We are all shaped and informed by our families and communities, so we only know what we see and what others teach us. Growing up we didn't have the world wide web, we had two channels on the television and if you were lucky a set of encyclopedias. I grew up with the belief that poor was normal and brought that belief into my adult life. A sense of 'lacking' in enough money, education, confidence and many others things to be able to make a life worth living. Of course, this was only my conditioning and all things can be changed once we decide or choose to do so.

I had decided to make a change and in doing so would allow me to heal any of my ancestral issues. This occurred very easily as I felt that I had been working so deeply on myself, it had allowed me to uncover many of my own truths and what no longer resonated with me from my younger life. I found that beliefs I had carried all of my life to that point, were not always my own, but ones that we had been taught to believe in, I wanted to believe in more than just what others told me. I wanted to experience to believe.

So, I started on my journey of healing with my ancestors. It was an amazing experience. I felt my ancestors lining up outside my back garden and queuing as if for miles and miles, they went back as far as Asia, which has now been proven by my Mother having DNA tests done very recently. I felt so honoured to have all of these wonderful people in my lineage and that they were now willing to help me shift the perception of their past from my energy so that I could learn a new way of perceiving the world for myself. Not all of their values were being shifted. Some were the foundation of our society, love, peace, understanding, acceptance and freedom for all, equal rights and free will, kindness to all. Simple but some of the most important values we hold within our human race that have been forgotten.

Through this beautiful ancestral healing, I felt the expansion of energy in that there was more to do, so I chose to set up an evening in a centre where I would do an Ancestral healing evening, it was amazing. So many people turned up and as I guided them through the healing, you could see the energy in the room heavy at first, grow lighter and lighter as we lifted the veil of illusion from our hearts and our minds. It was like watching a silent miracle unfold. We were not only healing the issues we were carrying from our own lives as a result of our family's energy carried down, but also healing issues that date back hundreds of years for many people linked to this group.

When everyone returned from the experience back to physical awareness, the stories they told were spine tingling. Some felt, or had seen their grandparents or further back, and what they had endured and carried secretly with them all through their lives without ever speaking of it. They thought by being silent it would never affect anyone, but in doing so their energy was shrouded in secrecy and energy does not need to be heard but is felt by all. It was revealed to us that they did the best they could at a time, that was their understanding of how things were. They now know better as they have long departed this earthly world and see that we may be carrying some of the same issues with us in this life, they want to help lift the burden of past pains.

What was only going to be one evening of Ancestral healing, turned out to be 10 evenings and then a few weekend workshops. People came from all over as they had not heard of anyone else doing this work except for a priest in Co. Galway. He would say mass and bless each person during it to bring healing to them and their ancestors, many reported a lightness and freedom afterwards, the same was happening at my groups. But they were not asking anyone to fix it, they were taking part and experiencing the healing first hand, they were taking responsibility and action to heal old wounds not only for themselves but also for their ancestors who didn't have that opportunity.

It became apparent that our past is energetically carried into our present lives and would ultimately affect our future. To me there is no separation between our past, present and future.

We are a product of past choices, decisions and learning. Our future is created by choices we make in each day and the values and beliefs we carry with us from our yesterdays. Space and time are simply the mind's tools for putting everything together. Energetically, our past is just held within our memories, our present is made up of each moment and moments today will create our future tomorrows. Each thought and decision we make in each moment determines what happens next, so all we have is this moment.

I realised from those first ancestral healing evenings that we all have options even if we were not aware of them, we could shift the energy of the past in our present time and thus our future was already starting to become what we wanted in that moment. To change a thought within each moment, to feel the emotion within your heart and to really connect with yourself and the Universe in that moment, everything was possible. We were seeing time as a linear concept, where it is seen as a series of events that are leading to something, beginning to an end. But in fact there is no beginning and no end to energy, it exists throughout time and space, it is infinite. So too is our beautiful energy, our physical body is only the protective casing for an everlasting energy fully conscious and aware at all times, even after physical death.

This taught me more as I worked with those that had already physically departed this life, they were still existing energetically. The past, present and future run parallel to each other. I am a product of my ancestors, no matter what their stories may have been, I now carry the positive attributes that each and every one of them have acquired over their living years and in some cases what they have learned after they departed this physical world.

CHAPTER 15

People Teach you Every Day

From the moment we are born, we start to learn from the people around us, we imitate other people's interpretations of what it is to live, be and feel. The people that shape our lives from those early years are passing on the knowledge and understanding they have at that time and also the information that has been passed down to them by generations before them, we all have our own twist on life. As a child you only learn from your immediate surroundings. I was no different.

I believe that people teach us so much, not just about life but also about ourselves. When we are taught what to believe, how to speak, what to say and how to act from an early age, we do so willingly, as we are unaware of any other way until we venture out in the world of school and start to experience life in different ways. We start to question things and that is when children start to use the word 'why' so often. They want to know why the world works the way it does as they make sense of all that is happening around them. I don't think I was an outwardly curious child with hundreds of questions, most of mine were in my head and I liked to ponder them and make sense of them in my own way and time.

I am very different now. I tell everyone how curious I am, it is an interest in people and in the world that fascinates me. I know we can't have an answer for every question but the fun is in finding out.

The world is made up of so many different personalities; it is our uniqueness that makes us stand out from others. I relish in the achievements and successes of others, I believe that when we value the work of another and their successes, you are also valuing yourself.

As my work is expanding, I am coming into contact with more and more people from all walks of life, each one offering me a great learning experience in how I can help them and find ways to work with what suits their energy and their life situation at the time. But I had a learning of a different kind to learn also. John had told me for years that I am too soft and too giving and I know he didn't mean it in a bad way, but he could see that I would give everything to everyone else before I would give it to myself. I did this in many areas of my life, in my friendships but also in my work life. I know that John has the biggest heart of all, but he knows when to say no!

Initially, when I started working with individual clients, it was easy to keep in touch with them and help them whenever they needed it. I was very friendly with all the people from my groups and we all had a lovely connection together but what I needed to learn were boundaries and it was going to be a hard lesson to learn. No matter what time day or night it was I was getting texts and calls from people, and being me, I always had to answer them so not to let anyone else down. In doing this, I was starting to feel very tired, it was not the fault of the people texting or calling as they were coming from a place of needing to understand what was going on for them and I was always available.

I always remember someone saying *"you are great Sharon, you always reply immediately."* I had not set up boundaries in my working life and because I was now self-employed, it became 'open all hours' in my mind. I remember my phone being left in the kitchen and the non-stop beeping, it was like a constant sound in the background of my life. I felt guilty if I turned it off or onto silent for even just a little while and always felt I should reply just to let the person know that they were being heard. I suppose in a way it was coming from a place within myself where I felt I had no one to listen to me.

From 2008 my work life began to get busier and busier and the phone was really starting to become the bane of my life. I remember sometimes wanting to throw it as far away as possible because the constant noise from it was really starting to irritate me. I would think about not replying to texts or calls but at the same time I would then worry about the person, and which was worse, the noise of the phone or worrying about someone being okay. To me, it was always the person that won, but I had forgotten about one person – me!

So big lesson to learn, one night in bed, the phone beside me starts to beep and continues to beep several times. I thought no one would text this hour of the night unless there was something drastically wrong, so I picked it up to check. It was a person that had a few glasses of wine and wanted to unload everything they were feeling in that moment and they knew I would listen. I got it, I was too available and open, allowing people to believe that I was always there when needed. It took a few of my close friends to tell me that no matter what profession people are in, there are working hours and anything after that will have to wait until the next business day.

So I started to switch my phone onto silent when I was taking a break, having dinner in the evening and also when it was family time with my kids as they had commented to me that I was always on the phone. I now didn't have the constant beeping in the background and I was allowing myself to give space and time to me too. I realised that you can't give everything to everyone, there is only so much that any one person can receive from you, they too need to learn from themselves.

As my life and work became much busier I had to learn to detach from my clients and groups and allow them to take responsibility for their own lives even if they were my clients. I know that some people may have resented the fact that I was in their eyes 'too busy' to see or talk to them but they didn't realise that they were not the only ones wanting that time and attention too, I didn't have the energy to deal with it all. I had to start placing boundaries for myself but also for my clients. I felt the backlash from some people and because I am so soft I took it personally. I was once told that I was getting too ambitious in wanting to share my teachings with as many people as possible, that I should stay 'small scale - it suited me better.' No, it suited them better, then I would be more readily available whenever they needed me. I soon realised that I was living my life by the approval and needs of others and it was not serving me well.

I learned a lot from a wonderful teacher Mr. James Van Praagh, Medium, Teacher and Author from America who was visiting Dublin to run a week long workshop that myself and a few friends attended. I was in my element, this man whom I had looked up to for so many years and read all his books, was now physically standing in front of me sharing his experiences and teachings with us. He taught us to stand in our own power and to work from that place of belief and confidence within oneself and ones abilities.

The proof of my learning was when he asked me to stand up in front of a few hundred people from all over the world and demonstrate my mediumship to him and everyone in the room. This was the most frightening and exhilarating experience of my life. I had used my mediumship with my clients, in my small groups and in workshops over the years, but this seemed bigger. I remember standing there and my legs began to shake. I could feel the heat rising in my chest and my heart started to pound. I took a deep breath, grounded myself and brought my attention to my solar plexus.

I stood firm and told myself silently *'I am standing in my power,'* my power was a belief in myself and a deep love for who I was in that moment. I recall saying to myself *'the people in the room are not here to judge but to celebrate your abilities as they want to celebrate their own.'* I simply asked any loved ones in Spirit that were present at that time to let me know if they wanted to pass on messages to anyone in the room and out it came, it was so easy once I just opened my mouth and spoke.

Of course, once I was finished I was shaking with excitement. With a little encouragement from my friends, I had gone up and done what comes so naturally. James van Praagh came up to me afterwards and told me I was amazing and asked if I had been training for years. I smiled and answered him *"all my life."*

This one big leap for me brought many things in to perspective, no one will judge you unless you judge yourself.

What you portray to the world is all that they will see and know, if they believe anything else about you then that is their problem and not yours. What other people think of you is none of your business, a lovely quote from the wonderful James Van Praagh.

I firmly believe that we look for the approval of others too much in our lives. I work from a place of love and understanding for each person that I connect with at each moment in time. I admire and respect the people that have worked their way up in life to become great successes in any area of life. We are all just trying to do our best and the reward is sleeping easy at night knowing, you did the best you could that day, helping the people that really matter and knowing that tomorrow is another day and we will face it as it happens.

You can't be all things to everyone. Come from a place of love and do what is best for you and in turn it will be the best for the people in your family, your friends and even the people you work with. The old saying of 'people come into your life for a season or a reason' is so very true. I have had met many people over the years that I have deeply connected with, some are still in my life and some are in the background, not forgotten but not necessarily as prominent as they used to be once upon a time. That is because at different points in our lives we resonate with different people. We learn and grow from our experiences good or bad with each person and bring with it the lessons learned from that encounter. Some people show you who you don't want be and others teach you who you now want to be.

I encourage everyone to stand in their own power of self-belief, once you can do that then you are enabling others to believe in themselves too. Cherish the people that support and love you for who you are, I do.

CHAPTER 16

Questions- Keep Asking

In one of my early meditations with Elepedro my spiritual guide, he introduced me to Thomas, an older guide who had a teaching quality to his energy. I sometimes resisted his teachings as he made me question my work and where it was going. I, of course was still doubting myself to a certain degree. I had faced so many fears at this point in my life that I believed or maybe wanted to believe that I was doing okay and that was enough for now.

But oh no, Thomas was encouraging me in a gentle but firm approach to move forward in my teachings so that I could help guide more and more people, I wasn't too sure and questioned everything he said to me.

I used to see Elepedro just sitting back and smiling as Thomas would endeavour to teach me to listen more intently to myself and to the ideas and inspirations that were coming faster and faster each day. I used to be a little cross at Elepedro for not intervening and allowing me to feel so frustrated, I know now that he was helping me to learn when we believe we are content that is when we should start moving and learning more and so I did. I had to come out of my comfort zone.

Thomas, in his own physical life, was a great theologian and had many writings in his name, this is what he told me. He had also taught me that his teachings were his beliefs at the time and only through his own research and experiences could he write about what he knew or understood. He said that many people used his teachings in generations to follow. He also told me that his teachings were of his time and that each person will write of their own belief systems to help and teach others. We all need a foundation to start with but that through our shared experiences in life we will learn that things change as does our understanding.

What it truly taught me was that each morning we awake to a brand new day and everything we believed yesterday can change in a split second. We are forever learning and growing and I was finding that out more and more on my journey of life. It was like pathways in the brain were opening up and I was discovering that the only limits in life are the ones we set ourselves, we have endless resources within and it is up to each of us to tap into them. I was now ready to move forward in my learning and to help others learn too.

This is what Thomas had been guiding me to do for quite a while but I had felt resistance to his teachings as it was taking me out of my very comfortable comfort zone. Stepping outside of yourself and showing the world who you really are is not always easy, but I knew that this was going to be my avenue to walk alongside others on their journeys.

I have met and worked with the essence of Jesus, Mary and many other Divine spiritual teachers. Their work on earth continues through us. To many this will sound strange but we can all experience this deep connection without being religious. It is within our understanding to connect with the energies that resonate with our thoughts and beliefs, so whoever you connect to is right for you.

CHAPTER 17

Resistance

S o, as I began to write out a plan of action going forward in my work and my life, I started to feel a little resistance. I meditated on this and observed where I felt it in my physical body. I wanted to understand why I was afraid of moving forward and how I could honour the feelings without pushing them aside only to appear at a later date. Fear is not real, it is built up by us over time and expands in our energy as we allow it to.

Once you face your fear and make it your friend, it will inevitably assist you in your greatest achievements. I remember reading Neale Donald Walsch's *'Conversations with God'* and him quoting this acronym of unknown origin F.E.A.R – *'False Evidence Appearing Real'* and it stuck with me. I like to change it around and say *'Feel Everything and Rise!'*

The start of our healing journey almost always begins when we believe we can't cope anymore and the fear of being like this forever starts to take over our every waking thought. The more energy we give these fearful and negative thoughts the more they grow into something real, but instead of learning to understand what those thoughts and feelings are and why they are there, we start to believe them. I had those thoughts for so many years and from time to time still do. I am very good at giving everyone else advice on what to do and need to remind myself on a daily basis to be more aware and listen to what is going on for me so I don't allow myself to get caught up in the negativity that comes so much easier than any positivity ever can.

This is what I too resist the most, having to look deeper within myself to see why I am feeling a certain way. Sometimes I just don't want to bloody look any deeper, I get angry and just say *'feck it, I want to stay in bed! I will deal with it another time,'* but after a little while when I calm down, I remember the feeling of being lost and alone in my thoughts and don't want to allow myself to go any lower. I literally have to push myself to move forward and to find other ways of getting my energy up and switching my thoughts just so I will allow myself to be with what is really bothering me. There is a huge resistance within our subconscious at times as we try to change the old ways of how we reacted to these fearful thoughts, somehow we believed it was safer to stay this way and it became our way of living. Now I know it was only existing.

I know the difference too well. When I feel the conflict I will get lost in it but then I work through it in meditation and go into that fear and the thought and feeling behind it. It is usually something very simple to start with but if I allow it to grow it will become so much bigger that I find it harder to find a resolution within my mind. Step by step is my motto, take it one moment at a time. What you resist, persists! So basically until you find out why you are resisting something it will keep showing up in your life.

My resistance at this time was to publish my book, to go out in to the wider public and let people really see *me*. To allow myself to grow even stronger and know that I can do and be anything I want in this life. I just had to choose to do so and remember that I don't have to do it altogether, it is just one day at a time.

But to do this I had to become quieter within myself and stop myself from being distracted by the pull of everything outside of me. I have said it earlier in the book, it is a battle within my mind and until I can feel the peace within my heart. There is sometimes a big battle!

CHAPTER 18

Solitude

During this time of resistance, I felt a need for solitude. My work had taken off at rapid speed for the past number of years and I was flying with it, but something inside was telling me to slow down. I was giving so much of myself to look after everyone else and again I was forgetting about my own needs.

I felt the need to retreat, not only from my busy schedule but within myself. I was a daily meditator and practised self-healing every other day, but this was just not enough. I simply wanted to just 'be'. I seemed to be *doing* all the time.

I know that the demands of family life and work were taking its toll on me and my physical body was now showing me that I needed to slow down and rest. Indeed, it had been shouting for quite a while!

I made a conscious decision to cut down on the number of groups I was facilitating in different locations and also reduce the number of clients I was seeing each week. It took courage to do this as with slowing down as it meant there was less financial security. This was a fear I had to face and trust that everything would be okay. This was my belief and I trusted my instincts that the decisions I was making now would benefit me in the future. I was teaching others to trust and believe so now this time I really had to listen to my own words.

We may never fully understand that sometimes we have to cut back in order to have more. I needed more ME time as it was a reconnection of my mind, body and spirit.

In solitude we find our deepest fears and inspirations. As I worked more on myself in this time, I found that I was fearful of change but knew that in order to help myself and others I needed to grow even more. This is where my now famous retreats came about.

I had a deep understanding of the healing that can happen within an individual and group sessions, but I always felt that we needed more time to go deeper. had run many healing workshops with different themes, the goal of each wa always to come away understanding yourself a little bit more. This is wher I was inspired to create my retreat weekends. Not only did I need solitude and time for myself, but so many other people did too. It allowed us to giv ourselves the time and space to create change without allowing ourselves to be distracted by our daily routine.

I have found the most beautiful retreat centre in Co. Clare, rustic and surrounded in nature. The bright workshop space is large enough to hold my group of twenty or more people. The room itself is octagon shaped, with large bright windows which look onto trees and blue sky and the light shines in from every angle so that we are immersed in light and nature.

To add to the weekend we have our organic vegetarian meals cooked for u and from the moment of arrival, we are made to feel that it is our home away from home. Everyone feels at ease and comfortable from the moment they arrive, each person accepting that they are joined by like-minded people, al wanting space and a willingness to discover a part of themselves that they had forgotten or to learn a new aspect of their now self.

We always start off the weekend with a welcoming or opening circle, each person introducing themselves and what they would like to get from the weekend. Some come with a definite idea of what they want, others are no sure but feel drawn to the retreat and hold no expectations, they just need time for themselves.

From doing these retreats a few times a year, I have realised that we do no give ourselves enough space to reconnect and because it is done over the course of a weekend, it allows you to totally switch off from the distraction of life and allow yourself to become more self-aware. The weekend retrea allows you the space to find balance within yourself, your life, family and work. It brings clarity and focus to what is truly a priority in your own life and if you do not look after yourself, you cannot look after anyone else.

Developing my first retreat was an amazing journey for me. I had put all my experience and learned knowledge into the workshops I would be facilitating over the weekend, but also the understanding that most of us simply want to relax and be ourselves. We want a safe place to explore our past issues and our future fears, to be listened to without judgement and know that we are supported as we bear our hearts to others. This was done through guided meditation, creative exercises, partner work, mindful walking, talking and listening.

The retreats started to become one of the main emphases of my working year and for many that attended. To this day, the retreats are growing in numbers and I recently invited outside facilitators from Ireland and the UK to join me in sharing their knowledge to help others to help themselves. In this way, it is not just the participants who are benefiting from the experience but also me. I, too, have learned so much from doing the retreats and it is a great honour to sit in the participants chair as opposed to the facilitators chair to realise that we all have so much more to learn, this way we are continuing our practise of self-awareness. I often smile to myself and say *"I am an eternal student of life."*

No matter where we are in our lives, we all need time away from our 'normal' lives, you may call this escapism if you wish, but going on holiday is a form of escapism too! The retreats offered me not only time away for myself to reconnect to just being me, but also allowed the other participants to explore their inner world and deal with issues that they don't have time to deal with on a daily basis, this is why so many people burn out when they decide to take a break from their busy schedules.

Any time I go away on retreats, even though I am working too, I find myself coming home with more gratitude and appreciation for my life, for my family and friends.

CHAPTER 19

Opening New Doors of the Mind

Being the *'eternal student of life,'* I am always curious about learning new things and allowing myself to explore new opportunities. For too many years, I had believed I was not a great student, but now I realise that we can't all be good at the same things and if you have a passion for something, you are more likely to thrive in that area. I know now that I am a great communicator, facilitator, teacher, therapist and hopefully a good writer!

The mind has always fascinated me and when I had happened upon an article about hypnotherapy, I read it with fascination and it stuck with me. As I am a true believer in 'no coincidences,' a few days later I see a post about a Hypnotherapy course offered in Mayo. I looked over the course schedule, work and qualifications it had to offer and something inside of me was saying *"just do it."*

Of course, I had a little self-doubt and said to myself *"maybe next time!"* I spoke to John and the kids about the interest I had when reading about the course and why I felt it would be beneficial not only to me as a therapist to add to my skill base, but also as I have a great fascination in the working of the mind.

My son Matthew just piped up, *"Mom, do it, you know you really want to and you will be sorry if you don't."* He had intuitively picked up what I was exactly feeling and thinking at the time, so that was enough for me. I immediately went online and booked myself in. I was very excited at the prospect of learning more.

Hypnotherapy deals with the injured part of the person's mind, not always seen or understood by themselves or others. It works with focused attention on the conscious and subconscious mind at the same time.

Mental health has become such a huge topic in recent years but it is still very much misunderstood. We can be labelled with depression, anxiety or some mental disorder, but no two people will have the same symptoms or reactions. My belief is working with the individual on what is going on for them right now and working with the subconscious to get to the root cause. Of course, it may have started many years before a sign presented itself, but with the help, guidance and support of a good therapist who they trust, it can be the start of their healing journey.

What I found fascinating during the study and practise of hypnotherapy is the amazing way our subconscious knows what to release in order to get well. During hypnoanalysis, your subconscious automatically brings to you a place and time that you need to acknowledge and understand as part of your healing process. We weren't born with anxieties, they are learned behaviours and belief patterns as a result of our past.

Clients look for therapists when they want to make a change, to make their tomorrows better than yesterday. They want to feel better, to change their emotional responses to the events of their lives and improve the quality of their life. This usually happens when they reach a crisis point and know that they can't continue with the way things are. They want to be happier.

From my own perspective, I can totally understand this. I wish I knew of all the wonderful therapies available to us when I was younger, but again I had to go through my life until I got to a point where it was do or die. I had to learn the hard way but I am grateful as it has brought me to this very point in my life. If I didn't have issues, I wouldn't have sought out the many wonderful ways in which I could help myself and others. I know I have travelled a path with many road signs guiding me along the way, all I had to do was to open my heart and my mind to what was and is best for me.

No two people are the same so each person responds or reacts to their issues very differently. This is where I am so intrigued with helping people, I want to get to the heart of their individual issue as I know my issues were based on not only the actual situations that occurred but my belief systems and thought patterns that I learned along the way.

I know that we have the potential for so much more and in getting to explore that is what fascinates me the most. I want other people to awaken their potential and to rise above being *'less than.'* Each and every one of us have the power within us to change the direction of our lives. I will be your guide along the way.

CHAPTER 20

Universe Delivers Dreams

For many years I had the belief that some of the many things I wanted in life were unattainable, that is because I did not believe in myself or that I was worthy of such things. I know now that we are worthy of everything the world has to offer. We simply have to send out the request and allow the Universe to return it to us. Sound too mystical for you?

It's not really. We are all made up of sub-atomic particles and what are they – energy! The world is your mirror; enabling you to experience the physical world in what you hold is truth, until you want to change it. Everything starts with a thought in the mind, how you develop that thought is up to you.

Throughout my earlier life, I wanted to be happier, feel more secure but based on the belief in my subconscious, I was held back by my own fears and doubts, so the energy I was sending out was returned to me in a way that mirrored my thoughts and feelings. As I healed my wounds of the mind, body and spirit, I allowed my energy to change, develop and grow. As my thoughts became more positive and my emotions were not so overwhelming, I had more clarity and focus in what I really wanted in life. I became a positive force of energy that brought about positive changes in my physical world. I was starting to create the life I wanted to live.

Clients often tell me that they really wanted something like a new job or to have a new relationship and it just wasn't happening. If, like me, they actually looked deep within and saw that their outside world will only reflect their inside world, they will have a better understanding and more self-awareness of why they are not attracting the 'right' kind of jobs/relationships.

Most people are looking for something outside of themselves to fill a gap missing within. You must first find out what that 'gap' is and then fill it yourself. This takes commitment to yourself and practise. Self-awareness and personal development is one of the most important basis for your whole life, when you know who you are and what you want, there is no stopping you. You will find new people and new opportunities 'popping' up all over the place, for many people they will say *"I just can't believe it, it is exactly what I wanted."*

If all you dream about right now is not good enough, it is a signal to you that you are not allowing yourself to accept all that you deserve in this life. You deserve the best. You have heard the sayings *"change your thoughts, change your world"* or *"be the change you want to see in the world,"* it is literally up to you. We are too long waiting for someone else to fix things within our families, our careers, our relationships, every change you wish to have in your life, starts with you. Once you create that change within your mind, your whole world will open up and all you have to do is open your arms and accept.

Now I see within different periods of my life how my thoughts, feelings and beliefs only brought about experiences that reflected my inner turmoil. Once I started to change my perception of life and recognised that I was the creator of my own destiny, I took my power, breathed it in deep and started to send out the energy of what I really wanted, one by one my world exploded with light and love. To me there is no denying that we are forever moving and changing and we must allow our own dreams to flow as far as possible, the world is truly your oyster.

CHAPTER 21

Saying Yes to Life

I read somewhere that if any opportunity presents itself to you, say yes immediately and worry about the details later. That is how I am feeling for the past few years. Instead of worrying about the how and why of something, I look at it from a perspective of learning and developing. I don't have to know everything about it right now, but I will learn as I go along.

I did public mediumship demonstrations to 120 people and also worked with corporate groups of up to 600 people, I stood in my power of self-belief. Of course I shook in my shoes beforehand, but now I know that is just my body's response to good stress and releasing oxytocin in my brain to let me know that it is preparing my body for this event. Now, I have an understanding of the physiological side of it, I just have to get my thoughts right. This has helped me in many cases where I had to work with large groups or sometimes just meeting someone new for the first time.

That is what writing this book has allowed me to do. There was a fear within me in showing my vulnerability, fear of not being good enough, again fears that had no real foundation, but learned fears going back to my younger years. I am not perfect by any means and certainly don't have life figured out. I am just like everyone else, where I shout at the kids, get frustrated at my husband, hate doing the laundry and never have anything to wear! I still have a lot to learn and a long road ahead of me but I am so looking forward to travelling it with the people that want to join me. I also love to dance, sing and express myself quite openly to those that want to listen.

In writing 'Saying Yes to life,' to owning my story and sharing it with others with the hope that it would help give a voice to the many people who still struggle to speak their truth, to face their fears and to maybe realise that their life is important and they deserve a chance at saying 'Yes to life' too.

I want my children to see me living my life, going out and doing what I love, but also understanding that sometimes you may not know what that is until you are ready. I have shared my thoughts and feelings with John and the children over the years and they have listened and sometimes laughed! I see my children now as young adults going out into the world on their own adventures, some I can only stand by and watch from a distance. I accept that they won't always need me and that is okay too. I know that my children in Spirit are growing too and will always be present in my life. I want to share my children's lives with them not to make them feel obliged to have to stay with their parents, I tell them that I may not be home when they come to visit when they are older, as I could be off travelling the world!

For myself and John we have allowed each other to grow as individuals. I see John still as the grounding force within my life as I still want to run off and do everything today! I am a dreamer and I always will be.

I had said at the start of 2016 that my life was going to change in that I was going to be more adventurous. I had stated that out loud and it was a strong thought in my mind and an even stronger feeling in my body. I had created an energy of adventure that was to show up in many beautiful ways.

Firstly, writing this book and sharing my story in my own words. Secondly, I wanted to see more of the world, facing a fear of travelling to somewhere new on my own. I didn't want to just go to a city and dothe normal sight-seeing. I wanted to experience a place by being present in it. And I found it right under my nose. A local company '*Into the West Adventures*' were taking groups on guided walks along the Camino de Santiago, it was perfect. It was everything that I had been thinking about. Long walks in nature every day, beautiful scenery and a presence of just going at your own pace. Evening meals shared with our group, lots of chat, laughter, dancing and singing.

In that group we formed a bond that we will all hold dearly for the rest of our lives, each of us were on a journey of self-awareness, maybe it was to push past our own limiting beliefs in that we can achieve anything if we set our minds to it, but mostly to accept ourselves just as we are and everyone else will accept you too.

Since 2017, I have walked four routes of the Camino de Santiago, each one a different experience and in ways I learned a little bit more about myself each time.

To also help others that were unable to make this trip, I walked on behalf of my local Multiple Sclerosis branch and raised funds for services in our area.

I have many invites and offers to work with more groups and corporate organisations in facilitating wellness workshops which integrate positive mental awareness in all aspects of their lives. It is being proven to me more and more these days, if you can recognise what holds you back, you will then realise it doesn't really have any power over you. You can make a friend of the one thing that has held you back for so long. We all need to reach out and ask for help when we are ready and when you do, you will never look back, only to see how far you have come.

As I now come to the end of my book, I don't feel relieved but actually very excited. All those earlier fears of revealing my inner most thoughts and feelings are not as prominent as I believed they would be. Some of you may resonate with certain pieces of the book, others not, but I know that some of you will also feel like you are not alone in the way you have felt or even still feel.

I am standing at the edge of the wild blue Atlantic and looking out into the distance. I breathe in deeply and fill my body with the fresh sea air. I am alive. Saying '*Yes to Life*' is my new affirmation, I want to live my life not just exist in it. I want to be part of every day and make it the best day I can.

I am safe, I am secure and I am loved.

Other Books by the Author

A 21 Day Gratitude and Guidance Journal.

Available from www.sharonfitzmauricemindfulness.com and from Amazon.

About the Author

Sharon Fitzmaurice is a Holistic Wellness Coach, Speaker & Best Selling Author. In her work, she combines all experiences from every aspect of her professional and personal life to help people to find and awaken their true potential. Like many readers, she too has come through her own struggles and challenges.

From an early age, she has been intuitively aware of people's energy and how it affects their physical, mental, emotional and spiritual well-being. Sharon believes in a holistic approach to self-care and has learned many therapies and practices over the years. These are now helping people to become more self-aware, more mindful and more positive in their daily lives providing more balance and an opportunity to live the life they truly want.

After years of her own personal development, Sharon now assists thousands of people in Ireland and online to implement the changes that will most benefit their circumstances and life right now. Recognising that each of us are unique beings and will not all think or feel the same way as anyone else, she works with each person in identifying areas of their lives they feel they need help with and then take it step by step through a process of self-healing, self-awareness, self-development and finding joy and pleasure in each moment. Sharon's mission is to awaken the light within you and open up a new door in your life. The greatest discovery will be of yourself.

Sharon offers her services as an Holistic Wellness Coach through the following services:

- Mindfulness classes

- Meditation classes

- One to One appointments

- Workshops

- Weekend Retreats

- Reiki Energy Therapy Training

- Group talks / seminars

For further details, Sharon can be contacted via her website at https://sharonfitzmauricemindfulness.com

You can also connect with Sharon via her social media channels.

YouTube: Sharon Fitzmaurice Holistic Wellness

Facebook: AngelReikiGalway

Twitter: AuthorTherapist

Please Review

Thank you for reading this book.

If you found this book helpful in any way, I would really appreciate if you would help me spread the message to others. Please visit Amazon where you purchased this book, or Goodreads, to write a review. This matters because most potential readers first judge a book by what others have to say.

best wishes

Sharon

Lightning Source UK Ltd.
Milton Keynes UK
UKHW020726041121
393369UK00009B/207